Endorsements

WHATEVER HAS BEEN YOUR EXPERIENCE with solitude, silence, suffering, and struggle you will be greatly encouraged by *Threads of Grace…A Survivor's Journey.* Through a compelling personal story well told you will be challenged in how to hold onto God while He weaves the beautiful and perfect tapestry of your life together. Not every thread makes sense and not every thread you would choose, but Melody leads us to rest and to trust in the Master who is working perfectly in your life. She will guide us in when to wait, when to act, when to confess, and when to praise. I think you will find it to be a real page-turner!

Dr. Randall T. Hahn,
Senior Pastor The Heights Baptist Church

MELODY DILLARD'S *Threads of Grace* is an honest and beautiful account of hope and survival. Melody invites readers into her personal story as she reveals how choices and unexpected circumstances led to the unraveling of some of her most cherished dreams. Through her own trials and triumphs she is refreshingly frank about why utter dependence on God proves to be the only solid foundation for her family amidst the ever changing landscape of life. Women will especially be drawn to Melody's story and her struggles with sin, cancer, infertility, and grief, and the faith that sees her through during the journey.

Kim Messer, Professional Editor & Writer,
Facebook.com/kimwrites

IN HER NEW BOOK, *Threads of Grace*, Melody Dillard weaves healing into hurt, help into heartache, and hope into hardship. It's a story of God's goodness and grace, and how His character, once woven into the fabric of our lives, will change us from the inside out.

Tammy Bennett
SBC of Virginia Women's Ministry Strategist
Author of 101 Make Over Minutes Quick Tips for Looking Good from the Inside Out *(Harvest House)*
Editor of WM by Design

Threads of Grace

A Survivor's Journey

Thelma,
God Bless!
Melody Dillard
John 11:40

Melody Dillard

Published by Cedar Hill Publishing
Chesterfield, Virginia
Design and printing services by Farmville Printing

The Bible verses quoted in this text are from a
New International Version (NIV), A New King James
Version (NKJV), or a New Living Translation (NTL).

Other quotations from Cowan, L.B. *Streams in
the Desert*. Grand Rapids, Michigan: Zondervan
Publishing House, 1997. Print. Whyte, Alexander.
"Alexander Whyte on Grace."
oChristian.com, 1999-2012.

Doctors' names in this story have been changed.

Order this book at www.livingbyhisdesign.com or
www.facebook.com/#!/MelodyDillardASurvivorsJourney

ISBN: 978-0-9893877-0-5

Dedication

THIS BOOK IS DEDICATED, with love, to my sister, Missy. Thanks to her continuous nudging and unending encouragement, you are holding this book. I love you more ...

Contents

Threads

Acknowledgements

TO MY HUSBAND, ROB, AND TWO CHILDREN, CALEB AND AVERY, where do I begin? I am not sure I can ever express the love I feel for you three. Nor can words convey my deep gratitude for your taking a backseat to this book over the last seventeen months. When I slacked in my duties as a wife and mother, each of you extended the measure of patience and grace I needed to continue pursuing this dream. Your unconditional love and support are what made this impossible endeavor possible...thank you.

TO MY MOM, MARGARET SHELL, my ever-present help in time of need. You have truly paid it forward over the last seventeen months. While I am forever grateful for your constant encouragement and willingness to read the manuscript one more time, I am most thankful for all your help in keeping my household up and running! I love you more than words can say and I am so glad God picked you to be my mom.

To MY DADDY, TOM GATES, thank you for always loving me unconditionally and making my childhood as close to the fairytale every little girl dreams of. I feel so blessed to be your daughter and I love you more than you will ever know.

To LINDA JACKSON AND SHIRLENE HARRIS, thank you from the bottom of my heart for listening to me talk incessantly about this book. I can't imagine my life without you two.

To MY OTHER MOTHER AND SISTER, SANDY DILLARD AND KARLEY POND, thank you for your constant prayers and encouragement, but more importantly for loving me like I was your own.

To ALL THE MEN AND WOMEN WHO SERVED AS FIRST READERS, proofreaders and prayer partners I appreciate the sacrifice of your time. I know how busy life can be, and I am honored that you chose to carve out time in your life to be a part of this journey with me.

To CAROLE NUNNALLY, thank you for sharing your God-given talent of painting. You beautifully illustrated the breast cancer ribbon on the cover of this book which is so symbolic of mine and Rob's journey. I am honored you were a part of this process.

To KIMBERLY MESSER, thank you for reading through the first rough draft of this book and being bold enough to tell me all the things I didn't want to hear but desperately needed to.

To OLIVIA WILSON, thank you for taking a very rough manuscript and polishing it into something amazing. You trimmed away all the excess and rambling, providing a sense of clarity and direction. And despite our bickering over all the grammar rules I have yet to understand, you still allowed me to tell my story in my own voice. I am so grateful God caused our paths to cross.

AND TO JON MARKEN, MY GRAPHIC DESIGNER, AND DAN DWYER, MY PRINTER, thank you for bringing my story to life in such a beautiful way. You made this part of the process more special than I thought possible.

Prologue

FROM AS EARLY AS I CAN REMEMBER, I had two dreams. The first, and most important, was to be a mom. I know that may not sound terribly ambitious, but I don't think I have ever wanted to experience anything as badly as motherhood. The desire was so engrained in my heart that the very thought it may not happen was devastating to me.

My second aspiration was to be a missionary. I am not sure that I really wanted to travel across the world to be one... my own backyard was good enough for me. I just knew I loved Jesus, so I set out to save the world. My neighborhood soon became my mission field and I would witness to anyone who would lend their ear. You know that child-like courage that allows you to share your beliefs unapologetically, unashamed and unafraid of what someone will think? I possessed that, and the determined, strong-willed spirit to fuel it.

The book you are holding is the result of what happened when those two dreams somehow collided. *Threads of Grace* is the story of my struggles to become a mother, as well as my testimony of God's unending love and grace. My sister, Missy, has actually been prodding me to write this book for a little over ten years. While I have always agreed there was a story to tell, I felt extremely inadequate given I am not a professional writer. However, in January of 2012, when The Lord impressed it on my heart to begin this journey, I knew it was time.

Trusting Him to make up for my inadequacy, I began writing. From that moment, I could see His fingerprints everywhere I turned. His leading and provision have been totally mind-boggling, opening doors I should walk through, closing ones I shouldn't, and creating a few where there were none. I have experienced more *God Moments* over the last seventeen months than I have in my entire lifetime. In fact, I even enjoyed a seven-day stretch of one unexplained miracle after another. God has indeed provided everything and everyone I needed to help me write this book. And it has all occurred in His time, in His way, and by His design.

When I first sat down to write, I wanted to share so many details about my journey through life with you. Desiring to describe what incredible parents God blessed me with, I yearned for you to see my mom for the servant she is and paint an intricate picture of my dad so that you would know I had a daddy and not just a father. I longed to communicate so many of the wonderful memories about my childhood that I cherish. But after months of praying and asking The Lord what He wanted me to share, I realized all those details, as precious as they were, diluted the real message.

You see, this book wasn't intended to illustrate how wonderful my earthly parents were, or portray what an amazing childhood I had, or even to prove how brave and strong my husband, Rob, and I have been through the years. It's not even my humble attempt to become an author. The real message written on these pages is meant to bring honor and glory to The Lord. I so desperately want you to see Him the same way that I do and experience His presence in your life the same way I have in mine.

As you turn each page and my story unfolds, you will see a life that is far from perfect. Just as the ribbon on the cover illustrates, my journey has left me feeling tattered and worn at times. You will clearly see all the many places and times I have stumbled in my walk as a Christian. I hope that offers encouragement and reassurance that, regardless of what your past may look like, God longs to give you hope for a new future. When I share how I struggled to let go of my pain and bitterness, I pray you will learn from my mistakes and instead *run* to the One waiting to scoop you up into His arms and heal your broken heart. As you read about my physical battle with breast cancer, I pray your faith in God will be renewed, believing that He is more than able to overcome any and every obstacle ... if only we trust. Most importantly, I pray you recognize He longs to have a deep and intimate relationship with you for all of eternity.

God Bless,
Melody Dillard

Foreword

"And we know that in all things God works for the good of those who love Him, who have been called according to His purpose." Romans 8:28 (NIV)

HAVE YOU EVER LOOKED ON as a master craftsman weaved a tapestry? Or watched your grandmother create a quilt from blank squares of fabric? Thread by painstaking thread these artists bring their stories to life in their work. Anxiously, we wait in wonder, curious what their labor will produce. Yet, no matter how much we wish to see the end result, it takes time for them to reveal their creations.

Our lives operate in a similar manner. God, as the Master Weaver of life, already knows how each of our tapestries will appear once finished. Nothing catches Him by surprise; each thread carefully passes through His hands first. Still, we can't know how our lives will turn out until we reach the end of our journey. Having already lived half of my life, I have come to appreciate that I wasn't allowed to view mine prior to living it.

For in my own humanness, I may not have chosen to accept the life presented to me. However, I also realize opting out would have been a great misfortune, since some of my sweetest memories were fashioned during the most difficult times along my journey.

Like many, I began crafting my own idea of what my tapestry should look like at a very early age. As children, we have idyllic notions of what we will become and what our future will hold. Some dream of becoming doctors and lawyers, and others aspire to become actors or musicians. And then there are those like me who simply want to be a mom. No matter how different our dreams may be, they each share one common thread. We all desire to live a happy and fulfilled life.

As a little girl, I spent countless hours playing house in my imaginary world. Imitating things I watched my own mother do, I would imagine myself with my baby, always a little girl, tending to all the things that a mom normally does: cooking, cleaning, and taking care of my daughter. I took special care to ensure everything was always perfect, just as it should be. But as I became an adult and pretending gave way to reality, my life was nowhere close to the fairytale I had envisioned in my childhood dreams. In fact, at the age of twenty-two, I experienced a tug on one of my carefully placed threads and my world began to unravel. At the time, I didn't understand why God would allow me to encounter such unspeakable pain, nor did I know how to deal with it. While I now understand trials and disappointments are simply part of life, more importantly, I realize our *choices* can, and do, determine how much heartache we endure along the way.

After much reflection, I recognize one particular choice that affected my life in a profound way, both emotionally and physically. This single choice triggered a string of events that spanned a period of ten years, and forced my husband, Rob, and I to face some of life's greatest challenges. Responding differently to each circumstance, sometimes we chose to trust God, but sadly, other times we did not. Hindsight is always 20/20 and I can see clearly when we failed to put our faith and trust in Him. Likewise, as I traced back over the details of my life, I also better understood God's purpose for allowing some of the pain and suffering. Though tattered and thread bare in places, I see, at least in part, the beautiful tapestry He created for me.

Each chapter in this book represents one of those threads and describes how God intertwined each one together to create my life's story. Naturally, there are many threads of joy — relationships and special people God placed in my life, but regrettably, there are also countless threads of consequences and disappointment. There are strands of love, faith, and hope that appeared and helped to break the hold that loss, grief, and despair once held on me. But most importantly, there are threads of grace. These are present throughout my life, often sustaining me even when I fail to recognize them. It amazes me how all of the various threads mesh together to help me better tell this story. Join me as I share some of my life experiences and how God helped me through them...when I chose to let Him.

Threads of Disbelief

Cancer. Millions of people across the country either have it or know someone who does. I never imagined that it would become a part of my tapestry in the way that it has, but its presence will remain throughout my life forever.

JANUARY 22, 2001. As my husband, Rob, and I climbed into the car to leave for the hospital that morning, the fact that I didn't get to have my normal glass of chocolate milk concerned me more than the idea that I might have cancer. In my mind, this surgery was nothing more than a minor inconvenience. Still, the thought of being put to sleep has always made me a little anxious. Staring out of the car window, I kept reminding myself everything would be fine. I was certain once they gave me the drugs that help you relax, I would feel much better. Honestly, I have always wondered why they don't give you those to take on the way to the hospital!

Despite all of my efforts to remain calm, by the time Rob pulled up to the entrance of the hospital, the butterflies in my stomach had upgraded to bats. My mind raced. What if something goes wrong? What if I don't wake up? What if I leave my child without a mother? And for the first time since we discovered the lump, I finally considered the reason I was at the hospital. What if it is cancer? What will I do?

Up until that point, I hadn't allowed myself to entertain such thoughts. Maybe it was simply a state of denial, or perhaps because we were incredibly busy in the weeks leading up to my surgery. January was, and still is, a hectic time of year for my family. We're typically still trying to settle down after all the holiday festivities. Christmas is my favorite time of year, and being an interior designer, I don't believe in doing anything related to decorating by half measures, especially where Christmas is concerned! I usually begin decorating right after Thanksgiving and I am still putting the finishing touches on everything Christmas Eve morning. By the time I am done, it looks like the North Pole has set up a satellite office at our house! And even though I wouldn't have it any other way, it always results in a lot of extra work for me come January.

However, that year with the date of my surgery looming, I soon found myself wishing I hadn't gone quite so overboard. I scrambled to get the decorations put away and thoughts of planning my son's birthday got pushed to the back burner. Caleb was turning five on January 18th, just four days before my procedure. Since birthdays are normally a big deal at our house, once I realized my mistake I was frantic to throw something special together. Needless to say, when Caleb asked if we could have his party at The Children's Museum, I was sure it was a total God thing. Expelling a sigh of relief, I couldn't make the call fast enough! I reserved the date, dropped invitations in the mail and checked it off of my list.

There was, though, one other minor detail contributing to my stress level. Rob and I were still trying to have another child. Having struggled with infertility for eleven years, attempting to get pregnant wasn't something we viewed as fun and stress free. We conceived Caleb through artificial insemination, and after experiencing years of difficulty we decided not to take any precautions to prevent getting pregnant again. Nonetheless, after years of trying... it simply wasn't happening. As we neared Caleb's 5th birthday, I mentally prepared myself that he might not ever have a brother or sister.

Even so, I continued taking my temperature and a little over a week into the New Year, it peaked. Rob and I knew all the signs to watch for. In fact, after many years of trying we considered ourselves pros at knowing what to do and what not to do. It looked like the perfect time to conceive... so once again we tried. That's the night Rob discovered the lump in my breast.

Given the fact I have never been consistent about performing self-exams, I wasn't even aware the lump was there. My annual checkup was in April of the previous year, so I knew it couldn't have been there longer than eight months at best. I didn't think it was anything to worry about, but Rob and I both agreed my doctor should take a look. First thing the next morning I called Dr. Elliott, my OB/GYN, and his receptionist, Cindy, worked me into his schedule later that week. Confirming the time, I pushed the end button on my phone and gave it little thought. To me, it was simply another addition to my already lengthy to-do list.

Driving to my appointment I made a mental note of all the things I needed to accomplish in the upcoming weeks. I was in the final stages of finishing up with a client I had been working with for the better part of eight months. Stretched thin, this actually felt like a waste of my afternoon. Arriving at Dr. Elliott's office, I signed in and took a seat in the waiting room. Within minutes Brooklyn, Dr. Elliott's nurse, opened the door wearing her usual smile and greeted me with a warm hello. Motioning for me to follow her, she asked about Rob and Caleb. We spent the next few minutes trying to catch up while I waited for Dr. Elliott to make his way to my room.

After examining me, Dr. Elliot explained the lump might be something called a fibro adenoma; basically, a benign mass. Sounded logical to me, since I was young and healthy and at the time no one in my family had ever had breast cancer. Dr. Elliott recommended I see a breast surgeon and have a mammogram done for further evaluation. I thought it was a good idea and was glad he wanted to play it safe, but I also knew this would require additional doctor visits. Cindy scheduled the appointments and I headed home even more relaxed than when I arrived.

At thirty-four years old, it was my first mammogram. Having heard many horror stories over the years, by the time my appointment rolled around I was a bundle of nerves. Shortly after arriving, all my fears became a reality. I quickly found myself harnessed into this contraption that squeezed my breast so hard I thought it would explode. Despite the number of images they took, there was no trace of the mass. I found that a little strange, considering Dr. Elliott thought it was about the size of a Peanut M&M. Thankfully, he ordered an ultrasound as well. It only took a few minutes for the technician to locate it on the monitor. There it was plain as day, a small mass in my left breast. After looking at the images, he agreed with my gynecologist. It didn't seem to have any of the suspicious signs that normally point to cancer.

We collected the images and headed upstairs to meet with Dr. Analise Truitt, the breast surgeon. Originally, I wanted to see Dr. Geoffery Caldwell, a surgeon well-known for this type of surgery. However, when I called his office to try and schedule the appointment, his calendar was full. In an effort to help, his receptionist recommended Dr. Truitt. I didn't know much about this doctor, nor did I think I had any preconceived ideas about her qualifications. But I must have, because as soon as she entered the room my comfort level immediately dropped. She was so young! Honestly, she looked like she picked up her diploma the week before. When I asked if she had ever performed this type of surgery, she laughed and assured me she had. We exchanged a few pleasant words and she began reviewing the ultrasound images.

Almost immediately, she agreed with the first two assessments. "I am ninety-five percent sure this is nothing more than a fibro adenoma," she told us. Even though I wasn't overly concerned, a third confirmation in our favor was a welcome relief. Since the lump was in the lower part of my left breast where the underwire of my bra would rest, Dr. Truitt suggested I have it removed for comfort reasons if nothing else. We scheduled the surgery for the following Monday and left her office totally at peace that nothing was wrong. With the exception of mentioning it to my immediate family, our pastor, and a few close friends, I barely gave it a moment's thought as we celebrated my son's birthday.

That is, of course, until we arrived at the hospital the morning of January 22nd and all the "what-ifs" began running through my head.

But even as I contemplated the possibility that I might have cancer, I couldn't shake another feeling. *What if I was pregnant?* Granted it was a long shot, a really long shot given mine and Rob's history, but miracles happen all the time. After all, Rob and I were together a mere ten days earlier, and by all indications I was ovulating that night. Aside from that, I honestly had no other reason to suspect that I was pregnant. At that point, my cycle wasn't even late. The thought continued to gnaw at me, so I decided to ask the pre-op nurse to administer a pregnancy test. Regardless of the fact I was sure it was a complete waste of medical supplies, better safe than sorry, I reasoned.

After eleven years and so many failed attempts, seeing a positive result was hard to imagine. I was certain this one would be no different than all the rest. In spite of this, when the nurse returned with a negative reading something inside urged me to ask if she would order a blood test as well. She was kind enough to oblige me without asking any questions. Of course, blood tests take a little more time to process, so she warned me the results may not be conclusive before it was time to take me down for surgery.

About that time, Dr. Truitt came in to discuss the details concerning the procedure. She explained to Rob and me that she planned to remove a section of the lump and have it biopsied while I slept. That way when I awoke, we could be certain it wasn't cancerous. After she finished going over everything, she asked if we had any other questions. While I didn't really have any concerns about the surgery, I did still have reservations about the anesthesia. And since the results from the blood test weren't back yet, I expressed my uneasiness to her. By this time, I am sure they all wanted to have me committed! In any case, she agreed to humor me and use something that would be safe for me and the baby… in the unlikely event there was one.

Finally feeling a bit more at ease, I was ready for them to start administering the "feel good" drugs into my IV. The last thing I remember before drifting off, I was having a benign mass removed from my breast and I wasn't pregnant.

However, when I awoke in the recovery room it was to a very different scenario. Dr. Truitt and Rob stood beside my bed waiting to talk to me while I fought to get my eyes into focus. Once I became more alert, Dr. Truitt wasted no time in telling me that she was wrong in her initial diagnosis. Not only was the mass malignant, the blood test came back positive. *I had breast cancer and I was pregnant.* I struggled to make sure I heard her correctly. Did she just say *cancer?* How could the mass be malignant? Cancer doesn't run in my family. Surely they had my biopsy report mixed up with someone else's. And *pregnant?* Rob and I hadn't conceived on our own in over eleven years; how could I be pregnant? There must be some mistake.

We were supposed to go in, have this tiny mass removed, go home, and get back to the hustle and bustle of life. Yet, with one simple word everything was different. *Cancer.* Certainly not a word I expected to hear at thirty-four years old. *You're pregnant.* A phrase I longed to hear so many times before. Neither was something I expected to hear that morning. Together they sounded unimaginable. How could this be happening?

But that wasn't all.

Dr. Truitt explained, "Even though we removed the lump, I am certain there are microscopic cells running throughout your remaining breast tissue. Your type of cancer is also estrogen receptor positive, Melody, which means this tumor will feed off the hormones your pregnancy will produce. It's a fast-growing type of cancer and we need to treat it aggressively." Dr. Truitt remained strong, careful not to show emotion, as she recommended that I terminate the pregnancy and have a radical mastectomy. She made it clear if I chose to continue the pregnancy, I would be lowering my chances of survival. Coming from her, it was as though she was diagnosing me with something as minor as a broken bone. The frankness in the way she talked took me back to a time many years earlier when another doctor delivered some devastating news to Rob and me.

Releasing me to go home, Dr. Truitt scheduled an appointment for us to return later that afternoon to discuss our options. As we left the hospital, I struggled to wrap my brain around the idea that God would allow this to happen. If He knew about the cancer, why would he permit me to get pregnant, especially after all Rob and I went through over the years? Why would I have to make a choice between myself and the child I carried? How could this be His plan? He is in control, isn't He? I even remember thinking, Okay, God, I can do the cancer and all the treatments that go along with it, but while carrying a baby? I don't know.

As I tried to process everything, I secretly hoped and prayed that my body would reject the pregnancy... it would just be easier that way.

"We were under great pressure, far beyond our ability to endure, so that we despaired of life itself... but this happened that we might not rely on ourselves but on God... He has delivered us from such a deadly peril, and He will deliver us again. On Him we have set our hope that He will continue to deliver us."

2 Corinthians. 1:8-10 (NIV)

Threads of Choice

Choice: the freedom to do things our own way. This one word holds the power to bring about many different outcomes in our lives, yet we don't revere it as such. Decisions I made as a young woman altered my life in a profound way, weaving in strands of shame and sorrow, ultimately teaching me the importance of choice.

WHILE I CONTINUED to mull things over, memories from our past consumed my thoughts. Rob and I endured so much in the ten short years of our marriage, this hardly seemed fair. Scenes from years earlier began to replay in my mind, and I pondered some of the choices we made in the beginning of our relationship, not to mention the choices I made as a teenager and young woman.

You see, like most young girls, I had always dreamt of meeting my very own Prince Charming. I wondered about his personality, his physical appearance and, more importantly, that first encounter between us. The idea of this relationship was huge for me, and though I contemplated many things concerning this part of my life, I failed to do the most important thing. I didn't pray about it, certainly not when I was little or even as I matured and really began to think about settling down with someone. I gave little thought to his morals or values when I was young. It wasn't until much later that I realized a man's inner heart and character are far more valuable than what he looks like on the outside.

And even though I grew up in a Christian home with two amazing parents who loved God, as I matured I did many things that resulted in less than God's best for me. My parents worked hard to establish a strong spiritual foundation, taking my sister, Missy, and me to church most every Sunday. Nonetheless, no matter how hard a parent tries, often a child's free will is stronger yet.

The desire to exercise my free will vehemently emerged as I reached the threshold of my teenage years. Even as a small child, I was always very determined to have things my way, but with age my determination only grew stronger. Maybe it was my way of coming into adulthood, or perhaps it was the underlying problems stirring in our home at the time. You see, just a few days before my freshman year of high school, my parents told my sister and me they were separating.

I will never forget hearing their words that night. Having watched so many of my friend's parents separate and divorce, I placed a tremendous amount of value on the fact that mine were still together. In my mind, we were the epitome of the perfect Christian family. After all, my parents never fought, at least not where I could see, and up until that point I thought they had the perfect relationship. If truth be told, it was what shaped many of my own hopes and dreams as a child. Being young and naïve, I didn't realize perfect families or marriages didn't exist. How can they with imperfect people in them?

Understanding that truth may have helped me accept their decision a little better; nevertheless, the idea that my parents weren't staying together completely blindsided me. Their divorce was my first real taste of disappointment, and to say I was hurt would be a gross understatement. Searching for ways to fill this void, I sought comfort in many things not related to God.

I am not sure my choice to stray away from Christian beliefs and values was actually a conscious decision, maybe just a reckless, immature one. Being raised in church, my faith in God was never something I wrestled with; I have always believed Jesus was real. However, during this time I in no way lived a life that implied that. I began looking for love and acceptance in all the wrong places. Regrettably, I wasn't at a point in my life where I looked to God for His input and I gave little credence to the effect my choices were having on my life as a whole. My search to find happiness continued throughout my teen years and into my early twenties, but no matter where I looked it simply wasn't there.

Then in the fall of 1987 my life took a turn. Still in college, I worked part-time at a local grocery store chain. That

November the store offered me a position in the accounting office at another location. It was there that I met Rob, my very own Prince Charming. I will never forget the first time I saw him. Tall, blonde hair, blue eyes, handsome ... you know the type. Aside from his good looks, Rob possessed a great sense of humor and was way too charming for his own good! He was kind and caring and genuinely respected others, something I hadn't seen in any of the other guys I had dated. If I could have placed an order for my ideal guy, he would have fit the bill perfectly. While we didn't have our first official date for several months, from the moment we met I was completely smitten; never realizing he was the man I would someday marry.

During this time, neither of us was attending church, but it didn't take me long to figure out Rob was a Christian. From the start we talked openly about our faith in God and it was clear we shared the same beliefs. Rob's family went to church regularly when he was younger, but their attendance eventually dwindled by the time he reached the age of five or six. In spite of that, his parents had managed to establish a good Christian foundation. A close family friend ultimately led Rob to the Lord when he was in his mid-teens. So even though Rob didn't grow up in church, he did have something I lacked. His parents were still together. Rob was blessed to grow up in a loving and stable home, made up of both parents and his sister, and it showed in the way he carried himself.

Our relationship was unlike anything I experienced in my teen years or early adulthood. Rob shared many of the same qualities as my dad; it was easy to see why I was drawn to him. I felt safe and secure, and I trusted him completely with my heart. Over the next few weeks, our feelings grew deeper and stronger. The weeks soon turned into months, and before I knew what hit me, I was head over heels in love with him and he was with me. There was seldom a day that passed when we weren't together. And even though we never really talked about marriage, I could envision us spending the rest of our lives together.

As our feelings grew deeper, so did our level of intimacy. When two people fall in love, resisting the temptation to become involved in a physical relationship is extremely difficult, especially when neither is seeking God's direction in their life. Intimacy is one of the most wonderful ways God created for us to express our emotions for one another; the only problem is, this relationship is designed to be enjoyed inside the covenant of marriage. Regrettably, we both crossed that boundary in previous relationships. Like most forbidden fruit, once you have tasted it, resisting the temptation becomes more difficult. That being said, neither of us considered abstinence as a choice.

I think that's actually where the hardships I faced throughout my life started. It's not enough to just hope you will remain pure; it has to be a conscious decision. Let's face it, if you are on a diet you don't pack cookies in your lunch and then pray that you won't eat them. Likewise, if you really don't want to become sexually active before marriage, you don't go parking with your boyfriend and expect to only kiss. This makes perfect sense to me now, but not so much back then. Clearly, I didn't give this decision the careful consideration it deserved. We both knew it was wrong, yet still chose to enter into a physical relationship anyway. As with most decisions to compromise one's beliefs, our choices soon caught up to us.

> "See, I set before you today life and prosperity, death and destruction."
>
> Deuteronomy 30:15 (NIV)

Our first Christmas together 1988

Threads of Consequence

There are always repercussions that follow the choices we make, whether good or bad. When our decisions are those that compromise our faith, the effects often bring with them consequences. I believe many times we bring on much of the pain and suffering we endure simply by not following God's plan for our life.

GROWING UP, WE HAVE ALL HEARD our parents caution, "If you play with fire you are sure to get burned." While I understood the dangers surrounding my choice, like most young women, I never imagined anything would happen to *me*. Still, given the nature of our relationship I was keenly aware of when my cycle should occur. Earlier that month when it should have arrived, it didn't. I noted it but wasn't too alarmed since I experienced problems with regularity anyway.

Rob and I went away for the weekend and after we returned home, I decided I should probably take a pregnancy test. No matter how old you are, an unplanned pregnancy is unnerving, to say the least. I was twenty-two at the time, and though I wasn't a teenager, neither was I married.

I will never forget that morning. Just buying the pregnancy test was scary enough, but actually going through the steps and waiting to see the results terrified me. You know that sick feeling down in the pit of your stomach when you look up in the rearview mirror and see blue flashing lights? Well, that's the best way I can describe my reaction when I looked down to see a positive result in the little square block on that pregnancy stick. Sheer and total panic consumed me. What was I going to tell my mom... my dad? Forget about them... what would I say to Rob?

I didn't know what he would say or how he would react. Having dated for over eighteen months at the time, I knew we loved each other, but a baby? *Now?* Rob and I had given in to temptation, and now we had to deal with the aftermath of our actions.

Somehow, this wasn't how I imagined my fairytale going.

Finally mustering up enough courage, I told Rob I was pregnant. Once the initial shock wore off, we began talking about our future. We both agreed we wanted to spend the rest of our lives together, but decided that starting out with a baby wasn't really ideal. Although I was working, Rob had graduated from college a mere five months earlier and was still looking for something full-time; we couldn't even afford to take care of ourselves, much less a baby. Terminating the pregnancy seemed like the only solution. After all, I knew other girls who made this same decision; it wasn't like I was the only one. Everything went okay for them, right? At least, that's what I kept telling myself. I don't think I even prayed about it, except maybe just to say, "Oh God, help me!"

Unless you have been in this situation, you can't possibly imagine all the things that run through your mind. Overwhelmed with emotions, I wanted desperately to do the right thing for the baby growing inside of me, but I also needed to think about *my future*. And then there were all the messages from the world bombarding me. "Take care of yourself, these are only cells. They aren't even a real person yet."

As I struggled to make a decision, I was completely engulfed with fear. I was afraid of what everyone would think once they knew Rob and I had crossed this boundary. But more than anything, the thought of disappointing my parents bothered me the most. Fear is a very real and powerful emotion, many times causing people to do things they never dreamed possible. I allowed these fears to convince me abortion was the only answer to my problem. Honestly, I believe this single emotion is what drives many other women to reach this same decision.

Even as difficult as it was to consider ending a life, I decided to call Dr. Charles Hamlin, my OB/GYN at the time, and make an appointment. His nurse, Linda, scheduled me to come in a day early to dilate me for the actual procedure the following morning. As Rob and I walked through the office door, our hearts were heavy, both uncertain of what we were about to do. I sat in the waiting room nervously fidgeting as I listened for someone to call my name.

Too soon, Linda opened the door, motioning for me to follow her to the exam room. As we walked down the hallway, I kept reminding myself that this would all be over shortly. Linda handed me a light blue cotton gown, asked me to undress, and said she would return in a few minutes. My hands trembled as I struggled to tie the strings on the gown. Lying on the examining room table waiting for Linda to return, my emotions were all over the place. Part of me wished she would hurry and come back so I didn't have to be alone, but a bigger part of me dreaded the sound of the door knob turning. I know now those moments I spent alone were a good thing, but at the time they were almost unbearable.

I'd known Linda for years and though I didn't know a lot about her personal life outside of the office, I could tell she was a Christian. She was always very outspoken about her faith and relationship with the Lord, sharing openly how He helped her through difficult times. There is no doubt in my mind that what transpired over the next few minutes was completely God ordained.

Gently tapping on the door, Linda asked, "Are you ready?" I answered yes, knowing nothing could be further from the truth.

From the moment she entered the room, I found it impossible to hold my emotions in check. Tears began streaming down my face, one after another, until I was sobbing uncontrollably. Just minutes before, it felt like I carried the weight of the world on my shoulders. Now, surprisingly, there was an amazing sense of relief coming over me. Somehow, from some unknown place, words began to flow from my mouth. It was as unrehearsed and unplanned as this pregnancy. In those next few moments, I seemed to have no control over what I said.

Through tear-filled eyes, I told her that I knew God wouldn't put more on Rob and me than we could handle and I really didn't want to go through with the procedure. Pouring my heart out to her, I expressed how much Rob and I loved each other. She listened as I talked, taking my hands in hers. To this day, I can't remember someone holding them so tightly. When I finished rambling, she wrapped her arms around me and prayed with me as I continued to cry. I know she wasn't an angel in the spiritual sense, but she sure felt like one that morning. It was as though God placed her there especially for me.

I got dressed, she helped me gather my things, and I walked back to the waiting room. Nervously, I looked at Rob and told him that I didn't expect him to marry me, but I couldn't terminate this pregnancy. We left the doctor's office both scared and uneasy about our future. Rob drove to a local restaurant and we talked about what to do next. Both of us sat at the table, pushing our food around on our plates, totally at a loss for words. After a couple of hours, we decided to tell our families that we were getting married and having a baby.

A week earlier I was sure it had taken all the courage I

could find to tell Rob I was pregnant; now, how was I going to tell my mom? As I got ready to break the news to her, I realized it would be even more difficult than I imagined. Thankfully, I have always known that my parents love me unconditionally, with a pure and simple love … no strings attached. Unconditional love is an immeasurable gift, one I was exceptionally grateful for that day. Even so, no girl is ever excited to tell her mom news like that, especially a mom who has convinced herself that her daughter wasn't even sexually active yet!

Before calling her to my room, I turned out all the lights so she couldn't see my face. She came and stood in the doorway and I asked her if she would lie beside me on my bed. After what seemed like an eternity, I finally forced the words out of my mouth.

"Rob and I are getting married and having a baby."

"Now?" she responded in confusion. We lay there in total darkness, as I couldn't even bring myself to look at her.

The conversation went back and forth with her asking me questions and my responding as best I knew how. It was an uncomfortable time for both of us, but at least that part was behind me. Next was my dad. Since he was living in Florida at the time, I actually told him over the phone. It helped not having to look him in the face. However, as a parent now, I am not sure anything could soften the blow for him or my mom. In my heart, I was so ashamed of what I had done and believed I had let them both down.

And telling Rob's mom and dad wasn't any easier. Sitting

on the sofa in their family room, my knees trembling, I vaguely remember Rob explaining our decision to his parents. I carefully kept my head down most of the time as I didn't want my eyes to meet theirs. The room was filled with emotion and I knew they, too, were disappointed. After all, no parent's dream is for their child to start out their adult life with a baby on the way.

At first, Rob's mom expressed reservations about us planning a wedding; she thought it was better to have something small and private given the circumstances. Though I understood there may be talk and speculation, I wasn't about to forfeit my wedding day. I had dreamed of that moment since I was a little girl. Even though I wasn't proud of what Rob and I had allowed to happen, I still wanted to experience the excitement of being a bride.

As I reflect back now on how I'd wanted the room to be dark when I told my mom, and how I couldn't look Rob's parents in the eyes, I realize that is really what sin does. It brings heaviness and darkness into our life. The shame I experienced was directly related to getting caught up in a lifestyle of sin. Rob and I chose to take a path other than God's best for us, and as a result a thread of consequence made its way into our tapestry.

Our fairytale had taken an unexpected detour.

"Then, after desire has conceived, it gives birth to sin; and sin, when it is full-grown, gives birth to death."
James 1:15 (NIV)

Threads of Uncertainty

With a baby on the way and becoming husband and wife, Rob and I embarked on this new chapter of our life full of hope and excitement for what the future would hold. However, things quickly changed, as they often do. Nothing could have prepared us for what waited just ahead as threads of uncertainty made their way into our tapestry.

IT WAS THE FIRST PART OF NOVEMBER and the next few weeks were a flurry of one decision after another. Planning a wedding in five weeks was not an easy task. There were countless details to address: invitations, the cake, flowers, the wedding party, finding a church, and of course ... the dress. With little time to spare, finding a dress proved to be a bit of a challenge. After the shock subsided, our family pulled together and all the details seemed to fall into place. My parents went the extra mile to ensure I had the wedding I always dreamed of as a little girl.

December 16, 1989, Rob and I became husband and wife, beginning a new chapter in our life together. We rented a small brick rancher from Rob's Uncle Tim and set up housekeeping. With me settled in my job, Rob still searched for something full-time. Things were tight and there wasn't a lot of money to spare, but this next phase in our life thrilled us nonetheless.

Given the fact Rob and I both still lived with our parents until our wedding day, there was a bit of an adjustment being newly married and expecting a baby. Thankfully, I had my mother as a role model to show me how to fulfill these new duties in my life. Meticulous in the way she took care of my sister and me, she established a perfect example of all the things a mother should do. Before long I was cooking, cleaning, and folding laundry; I had officially become my mother!

Along with settling into my new role as a wife and home-maker, the idea of *actually being a mother* excited me more every day. Dr. Hamlin had stopped delivering babies a number of years earlier, and at the time it wasn't really a big deal to me. However, now that Rob and I decided to continue the pregnancy, it was a huge problem. I needed to find another OB/GYN and quickly. Dr. Hamlin referred us to a female colleague of his, Dr. Stacey Sloan. While disappointed he wouldn't be the one delivering our baby, I scheduled our first appointment, eager to begin the prenatal experience.

Having seen Dr. Hamlin for years, I was comfortable with how he did things and I knew changing doctors would be an adjustment. I just didn't know how much! From the start, Rob and I were less than thrilled with Dr. Sloan. Her bedside manner left much to be desired and there was definitely nothing warm or fuzzy about her. Bedside manner may not be a big deal for everyone, but it is extremely important to me. Especially since this was my first pregnancy and I was oblivious about what to expect, I wanted and needed a little extra TLC.

During my first visit, she was unusually rough as she performed my pelvic exam. I thought it a little strange that she even chose to do that type of procedure, but I was too intimidated to ask any questions. After she inserted the speculum, it felt more uncomfortable than normal, and I expressed my discomfort. She seemed a bit agitated and abruptly brushed me off, saying she knew it might be painful, but I would be fine. When we left her office that afternoon I was furious, even telling Rob I wasn't sure I wanted to continue seeing her. At first, I wondered if I was being too dramatic, but that's when our situation took a downhill turn.

Within a few days of that first examination, I started to experience complications. It began with some light pink discharge and I wasn't exactly sure what that meant. Up until that point, the pregnancy was progressing well, so the thought that something might be wrong surprised me. In fact, my twenty-week ultrasound fell during the same week as our initial visit, and everything looked completely normal. I called Dr. Sloan's office right away to alert them. Since there was no sign of blood, she suggested I stay off my feet to see if it subsided.

Rather than improving, the amount of discharge drastically increased. Once again, I called her office and explained the situation to her nurse, Sarah. After talking with Dr. Sloan, Sarah phoned in a prescription for a yeast infection. She suggested I try that first, and if the medication didn't help to call back in a few days. Never having suffered from yeast infections, I couldn't imagine how this could be the problem. Nonetheless, I determined that I knew very little about the situation and since she was the doctor, I followed her advice. Upon finishing the three-day course of medication, I started producing gobs of thick white mucus, eventually losing my mucus plug completely.

Naturally, I had no idea what a mucus plug was, or that it was relatively important that it stay inside my body to protect the baby. I was only twenty-two weeks into the pregnancy when all of this started to unfold. I couldn't help but wonder if these problems resulted from Dr. Sloan's roughness during that initial examination. By this time, I wished I had followed my own instincts instead of putting my trust in her.

Switching doctors midstream in a pregnancy is stressful enough, but when you're facing a serious situation like this, it's overwhelming. Still, I knew making the change was inescapable, so we turned to friends and family for advice. A close family friend recommended her OB/GYN, Dr. James McClellan. I called right away and made an appointment with his receptionist, but just days before that date arrived, the light pink discharge changed to blood. Given the fact all of this occurred late one Sunday afternoon, when I called Dr. McClellan's office, the answering service immediately connected me to the on-call receptionist. She informed me that Dr. McClellan was out on vacation, but his partner, Dr. Tim

Elliott, was seeing his patients. I didn't know anything about this other doctor, but we really weren't in a position to keep looking. I gave the receptionist all the necessary information and she assured me the doctor would call shortly.

Within minutes the phone rang and it was Dr. Elliott. Unlike Dr. Sloan, he spoke in such a gentle way that he immediately put me at ease. After I explained the situation, he told Rob and me to come straight to the emergency room and he would meet us there. They admitted me to the hospital that night; I was a little nervous, but still not aware of the seriousness of our problem.

They promptly did a full series of tests, including blood work, a pelvic exam, and an ultrasound to determine the source of my troubles. The ultrasound images showed my placenta had implanted low in my uterus. No one had mentioned anything about a low placenta during the twenty-week ultrasound just two weeks earlier. I wondered if they noticed it, and if they did, why didn't they say anything? The whole thing seemed odd, but I dismissed it, relieved I could at least get the help I needed.

Dr. Elliott tried to explain the gravity of my condition. Pointedly he told me, "Melody, you are going to be here for a while. In fact, if you were my patient, you would stay in the hospital until you reached a safe place in your pregnancy."

Though I appreciated his caution, I was only twenty-two weeks pregnant when they admitted me. The thought of spending eighteen weeks in the hospital didn't sound very appealing to me.

Nine days later when Dr. McClellan returned from vacation, I actually felt a little sad. I'd grown rather fond of Dr. Elliott and I was sorry that he wasn't going to be my doctor. I even contemplated asking if I could stay with him instead, but I didn't have the courage to voice it. You know, the whole doctor/patient intimidation thing. Big mistake!

Dr. McClellan made his rounds that morning and came in to see me. We talked for a few minutes, trying to get acquainted since we hadn't even met yet. Of course, I expressed my desire to go home, and after examining me he agreed to release me. Having never been away from my family for any length of time, after nine days his words were music to my ears. Dismissing Dr. Elliott's recommendation for me to stay put, I didn't really see the difference in me lying in a bed at the hospital or at home. I certainly didn't think that anything would happen to me or my baby.

Dr. McClellan sent me off with strict instructions: complete bed rest. The only reasons he allowed me to get up and move around were to eat, shower, and to go to the bathroom. After talking about things, Rob and I decided staying at his parents' house would be the best solution. Since my mom worked full-time, she wasn't available to help out during the day, but Rob's mom, Sandy, had a more flexible schedule. Packing a few things, we settled in for what we thought was the *long haul*.

Just shy of the twenty-four week mark, Rob and I hadn't even taken our prenatal classes yet. I knew very little about what to expect in a normal pregnancy, much less one with complications of this magnitude.

I guess I would have to say, at this point, my ignorance was a good thing.

"But now trouble comes to you, and you are discouraged; it strikes you, and you are dismayed."

Job 4:5 (NIV)

Rob and Melody are officially husband and wife December 16, 1989

Threads of Helplessness

*Following this time of uncertainty, the helplessness I began to
feel was crippling at times. Nothing pulls at a mother's heart
more than to see her own child fight for its life... except, of
course, to realize she may not win.*

I WAS ONLY HOME FOUR DAYS when my water broke. A few
minutes before six o'clock in the evening, Rob's mother walked
into the guest room to check on me. I had been resting most
of the day and everything appeared to be all right. However, as
soon as I stood to my feet I felt something pop inside my belly.
As I walked down the hallway, a warm liquid trickled down my
leg. When I told Sandy, we both knew what had just happened,
but neither of us wanted to say it out loud. Within minutes the
contractions started and they were strong, coming about four
to five minutes apart. I called Dr. McClellan's office and Rob
raced to the hospital while I clutched a pillow to my stomach,
trying to control the pain.

As soon as we pulled up to the entrance of the ER, one of

the nurses met Rob with a wheelchair. She quickly ushered us into the hospital and down the hallway. The contractions were so close by this time, I worried I would deliver my baby right there. Once we were in the labor and delivery unit, the pace stepped up another notch. The nurses hurriedly hooked me up to the monitors to begin tracking the frequency of the contractions. Trisha, one of the nurses, tried calming my nerves as she started administering medicine in each of my arms. She explained everything carefully, telling us the injections were intended to stop the labor.

When Dr. McClellan arrived at the hospital, he walked over to the side of my bed, touched my arm, and asked how I was doing. Even though he could see I was in quite a bit of pain, he recommended I hold off on taking the epidural.

"It will permit your body to relax, allowing the baby to move into the birth canal," he said. As much as I needed some relief, I wanted to stop the labor more, so I agreed. Walking across the room, he took a seat on the sofa. Pausing only to wait for me to finish each contraction, he explained to Rob and me what we were up against. "This is too soon for your baby to be born. The longer we can keep him or her inside of you, the better. The lungs need more time to develop," he clarified, adding, "Given that your water has already broken, if we are successful in stopping the labor, there could still be complications. Without the amniotic fluid present, your baby is at a greater risk for infections." While his words frightened me, I remained hopeful that they would be able to stop the labor.

The contractions went on for hours, never spanning more than three to four minutes in between. Just before midnight, Dr. McClellan made one final check to see how I was doing. He seemed satisfied and headed home to eat some dinner, assuring us he would return in a while. It had been six hours since my water broke. Exhausted both physically and mentally, I asked Trisha if she could give me anything to ease the pain. Thankfully, she managed to catch Dr. McClellan on his way out and he ordered a small dose of morphine. When the effects kicked in, the pain immediately eased up, and it was a welcome relief. At first, it made me think the labor was tapering off, and for a short time, I had a sense of hope that the medication was working.

Shortly after one o'clock, I felt an excruciating pain in my stomach. Squeezing my legs together, I reached down and placed my hand between my legs. I could feel the baby's head! Rob called for Trisha and she came running into the room. The expression on her face told me it wasn't good. "The baby is crowning, it's coming, ready or not!" she exclaimed.

Trisha called for help and a man passing down the hallway entered the room. I immediately recognized him as the doctor who performed my ultrasound a few weeks earlier. The atmosphere in the room quickly changed. My heart raced and I knew it was too early. With an abruptness in his voice, he ordered me to push! Everything inside told me to do the opposite and when I hesitated, he immediately took both hands, and with one quick blow to the top of my stomach, our baby arrived. Instead of laying her on my chest for me to hold, a team of doctors waiting to stabilize her whisked her away to an incubator they had set up in the corner. It was a make-shift work station brought in earlier that night in case their attempts to stop my labor were unsuccessful. Rob and I looked on as they huddled around her. Once the doctors finished, our baby was taken to the Neonatal Intensive Care Unit (NICU). This moment was not at all what I imagined it would be like. And though I barely caught a glimpse of her, she was the tiniest baby I'd ever seen. Her size took my breath away.

Even though the doctors did everything humanly possible to stop the labor, I gave birth to a very tiny baby girl that night … tiny, fragile, and too soon. Leighton Elyse Dillard was born March 2, 1990. She weighed 1 lb. 9 oz. and measured 13 inches long. Complete right down to her eyelashes, she was perfect. Her fingers looked like tiny little matchsticks and her skin still had a transparency about it. The blood pressure cuff they placed around her arm barely fit around my pinky finger. She was so small you could have put her in a shoebox; yet, she was fully formed. Psalm 139:13 says, "For you created my inmost being; you knit me together in my mother's womb." That night I realized human life is truly nothing short of a miracle.

Dr. McClellan arrived back at the hospital shortly after the nurse transported Leighton to the NICU. Walking into the room, he made his way over to the sofa and once again took a seat. He wasn't typically warm or gentle in the way he spoke, his demeanor rather forthright and business-like. Dr. McClellan wasn't really the kind of person you would want to break this sort of news to you. In a very matter of fact manner, he told us things weren't good.

"She has come too early, and her chances of survival are low," he said. "If she does survive, she will more than likely have medical complications."

Of course, that's not what I heard. I heard, "Your baby is really premature and things are serious, but we will do whatever we can to get her healthy so you can take her home in a few months." I never believed in my heart she wouldn't make it. After all, this sort of thing happens to other people, not to me. My mind immediately went into a mode of denial; it was the best way for me to cope.

Once he finished, Rob and I waited anxiously for someone to return with news about Leighton's status. Dr. Carrington, the head neonatologist, came in shortly after Dr. McClellan left. Kind and soft spoken, his countenance was completely different and it was clear he felt compassion for what we faced. Dr. Carrington said he wanted to update us on Leighton and answer any questions we might have. His attitude offered encouragement as he assured us they were working to stabilize her as we spoke. Trying his best to educate Rob and me on some of the equipment we would see in the NICU, he explained the ventilator was designed to help Leighton's lungs function better. The information was completely overwhelming and I found it hard to concentrate on anything he said. I just wanted to see my baby.

It seemed like an eternity before the NICU called, giving the okay for us to head down to see her. I could hardly wait to make sure she was alright. Finally, one of the nurses came to let us know they were ready. Trisha helped get me into a wheelchair and Rob and I made our way to the unit to see our baby. Looking at her, she appeared fully developed, only in miniature size. But Dr. Carrington continued to emphasize her lungs were still extremely underdeveloped, thus presenting her biggest battle. I had to remind myself that she was sixteen weeks early.

In the days that followed, all I wanted to do was take her in my arms and hold her close. Close enough to smell the scent that only a newborn has; close enough to smell her breath. I longed to hear all the tiny sounds that newborn babies make as they stretch and wriggle. But from the beginning, there was no cuddling her in my arms. No singing and rocking her to sleep. No giving her the first bottle; the machines took care of that. Instead, I settled for swabbing her mouth with a moist Q-tip, or rubbing lotion on her back and arms whenever she had dry skin. The nurses and doctors stressed how important it was to keep her body temperature up, so we were careful not to keep the incubator open too long.

With each day that passed, we felt we reached a huge milestone and I found comfort in knowing we were that much closer to her being healthy enough to bring home. Still, every day presented a new set of challenges. We watched the monitors closely, sometimes taking one step forward and others taking a step or two back.

Of course, there were other babies in the NICU too, and we watched them carefully, comparing Leighton's progress to theirs. When Leighton's numbers matched the stronger babies', it offered encouragement and hope, but when her vent readings fell, so did our spirits. Although we knew little about any of the other families, we suddenly had an instant connection. We all hung onto the same thread of hope that our children would one day be well enough to go home.

Aside from the connection we felt with the other families, Rob and I also formed an undeniable bond with Leighton's nurses and doctors. I guess it started first with the respect their position commanded; after all, we were entrusting them with the life of our child. Dr. Carrington's kind and compassionate spirit showed through time and time again, as he handled our emotions tenderly. And as for Leighton's primary nurse, Alexandra, it didn't take me long to completely fall in love with her. She was full of life and she was as cute as her personality. Alexandra always wore a smile that stretched clear across her face. Whenever the hospital scheduled her to work, they assigned her to care for Leighton. If ever I had a question or concern, Alexandra was there, ready to help. I loved being around her; I soon found myself missing her when she wasn't there and thrilled when I walked through the doors and saw her hovering over Leighton's incubator.

There was something special about her; she was Leighton's guardian angel. She did something I longed to do...care for my daughter.

"The Lord is close to the brokenhearted and saves those who are crushed in spirit."

Psalm 34:18 (NIV)

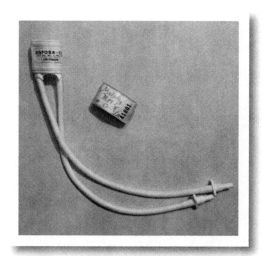

*Leighton's wristband
and blood pressure cuff*

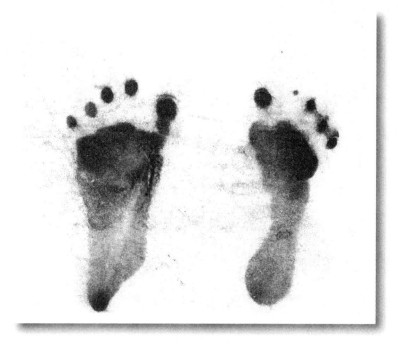

*Footprint of an Angel—
Leighton Elyse Dillard born March 2, 1990 at Henrico Doctor's Hospital*

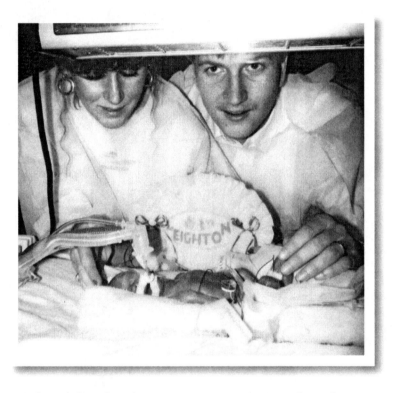

Rob, Melody and Leighton at Henrico Doctor's Hospital March 1990

Threads of Loss

From the moment I gave birth, I seemed to lose all control. My baby struggled to live while I stood by her incubator totally incapable of helping her. In retrospect, I understand that God had the situation in hand, but as a mother watching her child suffer, it was as though He had abandoned us.

NEARING THE TWO-WEEK MARK after Leighton's birth, we felt a little more at ease with her progress. We were at least able to decipher all the information the monitors provided. Her vent readings declined, which meant she used the ventilator less to help her breathe; of course, the goal was for her to eventually breathe on her own. That seemed a long way off, but just as any normal parent anticipates their baby reaching a new milestone, so did we … they were only different ones. Though they were guarded in their optimism, we clung to every positive word the doctors said.

After meeting with Dr. Carrington one afternoon, we learned they had discovered a heart murmur. He explained that this was very common in premature babies, and he told us it needed to be surgically corrected as soon as possible. Though I understood the necessity, it scared me to imagine them operating on her, considering her tiny and fragile state. Since he wanted to wait until she was a little stronger, we scheduled the surgery for March 20th.

That morning, Rob and I arrived at the hospital a little early to spend some time with Leighton before her procedure. In order to get into the NICU, we had to wash up and put on sterile clothing before entering the incubation area. There was a button beside the door for parents to push, alerting the nurses you were ready to come in. With everyone normally busy tending to the needs of the babies, I found it odd that Dr. Carrington stood in the doorway that day. At first, I assumed he was waiting to talk about the surgery.

As we got closer, he motioned for us to follow him into a small, private meeting room. I used this space several times before to pump my breast milk in the hope that, one day soon, Leighton would be able to drink from a bottle. He asked us to sit down and his countenance was clearly different. I could tell something was wrong and my heart immediately began to sink.

Dr. Carrington tried to explain that Leighton had taken a turn during the night. "We believe she has developed an infection and we have started her on a round of antibiotics. Leighton's color isn't the normal reddish pink you are used to seeing." He went on to say, "She doesn't look like herself,

Melody. When babies are sick, the first place it shows is in their physical appearance. Right now her skin looks gray, but as the medicine begins to work, her color will return to normal."

As I listened to what he said, fear enveloped my whole body and I could almost feel the air start to dissipate. Sobbing uncontrollably, I was now struggling to breathe.

We followed him into the unit and over to Leighton's incubator. Even though he tried to warn us, there really were no words to prepare our hearts for what we saw. With one quick glance I realized he was right, she didn't even look like the same baby. Gray and extremely frail, her coloring resembled someone who had already passed away. For the first time, she truly looked sick. Even though I knew she was premature and not healthy, up until that point she didn't appear that way. I viewed her as a normal baby, only smaller, but now I could see she was fighting for her life. Dr. Carrington explained that with the infection, she wasn't strong enough to undergo the surgery on her heart. We needed to focus on getting her over this hurdle first.

Even seeing her like this, I wouldn't allow myself to consider the thought of her not being here. I laid my hands on her chest and I prayed, asking God to heal her. It wasn't the first time I prayed that, but this time I pleaded with Him. It was the kind of prayer where you make any and every promise you can think of to God.

You know the one. "God, if you'll just answer this one prayer, I will never ask you for anything again."

Before we left that night, she began to regain her color, looking more like herself again. It appeared the antibiotics were working. Our spirits lifted, and I thanked God for answering our prayers.

Not knowing what the next day would hold, Rob and I knew we needed to get some rest. Heading home around 11:30 that night, we were physically and emotionally drained. Tossing and turning for the next few hours, we drifted in and out of sleep. Around 4:30 in the morning, the phone rang, startling both of us. The sheer sound of the phone ringing in the still of the night made my heart race. But even more than that, it told me something was wrong. Not wanting to answer, I reached for the phone and said, "Hello."

It was Alexandra. In a panicked voice she said, "Melody, you and Rob need to get back to the hospital as soon as possible. Leighton's not doing well and the doctors don't think she will make it."

Immediately flooded with thoughts ranging from disbelief to despair and fear, we called our families and asked everyone to pray. Rob and I were desperate for a miracle. The drive to the hospital, a good forty-five minutes from where we lived, felt twice as long that morning. By the time we walked through the doors, I could barely breathe; my heart literally ached inside my chest. Just a few hours earlier, we clung to a tiny ray of hope. In an instant, all hope seemed to vanish right before my eyes.

She had fought bravely over the last nineteen days; I thought things were turning around for the better. Now, all I could think was, "God, why are you letting this happen? With a single touch from You, she could be whole."

We walked into the NICU to see the nurse pressing two fingers on Leighton's chest just to keep her heart beating until we could get there. I couldn't believe her body was so tiny and fragile that such a small amount of pressure sustained her life.

Dr. Carrington met us at the door, clearly distraught. "She is extremely sick, Melody. Her heart stopped and even though we revived her, it took too long," he said. "If she does pull through, I am certain there will be serious complications due to the length of time she went without oxygen."

"What kind of complications?" Rob asked.

"Complications that wouldn't allow her to have a normal life: learning disabilities, loss of sight, loss of hearing, things like that," he elaborated. The list was long. In spite of everything he said, I still just wanted her to live.

Someone called for the hospital chaplain to come in and pray for Leighton. After he finished, he asked Rob and me, "Would you like me to baptize your daughter?" Nodding our heads yes, he went through the motions. As soon as the chaplain completed the baptism, the nurse stopped the chest compressions and the line on the monitor went flat. Leighton was gone.

From that moment, I am sure the events that followed moved very quickly, but I saw it all in slow motion. The nurses and doctors tried to talk to Rob and me, but I could no longer hear anything they said. It was like watching this horrific scene unfold as you looked on from behind a glass wall. I wanted desperately to pound on the wall as hard as I could and shout, "Stop! That's my baby, and I don't care what's wrong with her. I will take her, imperfections and all!" I wanted to scream, but nothing would come out. My heart was broken.

I stood beside her incubator watching in disbelief as they prepared to remove her from the machines that once sustained her life. Removing all the tiny patches that normally covered her body, they disconnected the ventilator. Dr. Carrington unhooked Leighton, wrapped her in a blanket and laid her in my arms... and for the very first time, I got to hold my baby.

> "So with you: Now is your time of grief, but I will see you again and you will rejoice, and no one will take away your joy."
>
> John 16:22 (NIV)

Threads of Grief

As I began the grieving process, I was now the one in need of healing. Grief, like a wild fire, can be consuming if not contained. Following any tragedy, there is always a need to mourn, but if you aren't careful, it is easy to stay there too long. I began to drown in my heartache and sorrow after losing Leighton as these threads wrapped themselves around me, slowly strangling me.

IN A SINGLE MOMENT, everything in our world came to a screeching halt. There were no more questions to ask, no monitors to watch, no wondering if she would ever be strong enough to come home. There was nothing … it was over … all hope was extinguished.

As they placed her lifeless body in my arms, I held her close and kissed her tiny face … something I longed to do over the last few weeks, but never envisioned it would be like this. It hurt more than I ever imagined possible. I desperately begged God, "Please bring her back to life, please make her breathe."

Frantically, I tried to remember pieces of the Scripture that tell us God can move mountains if only we believe. I cried out to Him, "Your Word says if we have faith as small as a mustard seed and ask, You will do it! Please heal my baby!" I prayed over and over that morning for God to make her heart start beating again. I believed He could bring her back to life ... if it was His will.

We left the hospital without our baby, and there really are no words to describe how I felt. Losing a child goes against the very grain of how we view life. There was now this hole in my heart, a void, a feeling of hopelessness that far surpassed anything I had ever known. Hurt and confused, I knew Rob and I made mistakes in the beginning, but we ultimately chose to do the right thing. Four months earlier we decided not to abort this child. We chose life over abortion, only to lose her anyway. Lying on the table in Dr. Hamlin's office that day, I expressed to Linda that I knew God wouldn't put more on us than we could handle. At this moment I wasn't so sure.

Now, instead of sending out birth announcements, we made preparations for a private graveside service. Since only a handful of people ever saw Leighton, we decided to keep it small, with only our immediate family members and Leighton's nurse present. I felt it was better that way. Honestly, most of what happened those first few days is a complete blur for me. I barely even remember meeting with the funeral director to make the arrangements. Until I began the process of writing this book, I didn't even know who took care of the financial burden of her funeral. There is, however, one thing I remember clearly about that morning. As I sat at the grave site staring at her casket, I remember thinking to myself, "I didn't know they made them this small."

Seeing how heartbroken we were after the funeral, Alexandra encouraged Rob and me to seek counseling. She told me that couples who lose a child have a lower chance of staying together. Statistics show approximately 75–80% of married couples who deal with the loss of a child eventually divorce. I listened to what she said, but really didn't take heed of it.

Twenty-one days earlier I had given birth to a baby. My body was still reeling with the hormones of pregnancy, and I found myself confronted with this unbearable grief. As our family left that afternoon, I replayed those final days over in my mind. I desperately wanted to go back to a time when she was still here. A time before any of this happened, when a flicker of hope remained, suggesting that I would one day get to take my daughter home. I remember wanting someone to shake me and say, "Melody, it's time to wake up," confirming that Leighton's death was only a bad dream. No one came to wake me and the reality of everything closed in around me. Leighton was gone. In all of my childhood dreams, I never imagined I would experience losing a child … not ever.

Rob and I were only married three months when Leighton passed away. We should have still been honeymooning, but instead we struggled to support each other as we grieved over the loss of our child. The fact that we mourned in opposite ways is not surprising at all, since God wired men and women's emotions totally differently. Rob held his pain in and tried to be strong for me. After the funeral, I never saw him cry again. Unlike Rob, I wore my heart on my shirtsleeve; I was inconsolable. There was no stopping me as I wrapped my sorrow around me like a blanket.

I watched everyone else's life resume normalcy while we picked up the pieces of our broken dream. Each day I struggled with the simple act of getting out of bed. I have never been someone who wrestled with depression or thoughts of suicide, but during this time there were many days I prayed the Lord would take me home so I could be with Leighton. Even driving to and from places, I sometimes looked at the oncoming cars and thought, "If I just crossed over the line it would all be over. My grief would end and I could be with my daughter."

Her nursery became my sanctuary, a place to mourn. With the room already decorated, I sat in the rocking chair and wept. Though we only had Leighton for a short time, I found myself pondering all the possibilities of her life. I wondered who she would have looked like, me or her daddy. Would she have been funny like Rob, or quiet like me? And even though I never heard the sound of her laugh or saw her reach for me to pick her up, I missed her. I soon realized I would never see her off to her first day of kindergarten, never watch as she twirled on her tippy toes or straighten her veil on her wedding day. I grieved over all of the "what ifs" as well as my baby.

A few weeks after Leighton passed away, I returned to

work. Walking through the doors that first afternoon was unbearable. My co-workers made welcome back posters, which they displayed all over the office. I could see they were broken-hearted, and their compassion surrounded me. They were simply trying to help, but I didn't want to be there. I didn't want to be anywhere.

In an effort to try and give me a fresh start, my manager transferred me to another location. While it seemed like a good idea at the time, because of the store's location, it actually made things worse. The store they sent me to took me right by the cemetery where we buried Leighton. On the second row from the road, if I caught the traffic light just right, I could read the words on her headstone. "For God in His perfect and all wise way chose our tiny rosebud for His heavenly bouquet."

Stopping most days after work, I put fresh flowers on her grave. Sinking deeper and deeper, I began to embrace my pain, as though it was part of my identity. If someone announced they were expecting, I wouldn't say congratulations, and attending baby showers was totally out of the question. I watched my two best friends finish their pregnancies and deliver healthy babies, the whole time wishing it was me instead.

No matter where I went, I came into contact with a newborn baby or a mom-to-be, only adding to my pain. It seemed as if the whole world was pregnant or had children, except for me. Despite everyone's efforts, no one around me knew how to deal with my choice to remain entrenched in my grief. Not even my mother. In an attempt to ease my sorrow she would say,

"Melody, someday you'll be able to help another mother who is going through the same situation. You'll get through this and be stronger because of it."

Heartbroken, I would cry and tell her, "I don't want to be the person who helps someone. I want to be the one who gets to bring my baby home." Convincing myself it was too hard to move on, I chose not to face the reality of our loss. At the time, I couldn't see that while *my suffering* wasn't a choice, *how* I suffered was. Grieving over any loss is painful, but there is a right and wrong way to work through the process. It can either be destructive or constructive. Our minds, and what we allow them to dwell on, are critical to how long the healing takes. In my own stubbornness, I chose not to put this hurt behind me. Rather, I firmly planted myself in my pain and bitterness and let them take root.

> "I am exhausted from crying out for help; my throat is parched; My eyes are swollen with weeping, waiting for my God to help me."
>
> Psalm 69:3 (NLT)

Threads of Disappointment

Feelings of disappointment soon became intertwined with my grief. And though I lacked the power to change my circumstances, I did have control over how deep I allowed my emotions to run. It was years before I finally realized this truth.

AS A MOTHER WITHOUT A CHILD, all I wanted was to try and conceive another baby. Rob, on the other hand, grieved in a very different way. We went through so much in such a short period, he thought we needed time to heal. While I knew he was right in many ways, I believed my only chance of consolation rested in the hope of another child. With that mindset, I persisted, eventually wearing him down.

After losing Leighton, I decided to change gynecologists. Given the way Dr. McClellan handled things the night of her birth, I knew he wasn't the doctor for me. Dr. Elliot treated me with such compassion and tenderness when I faced my complications with Leighton that I opted to start seeing him. Once he gave us the okay to start trying again, conceiving a child became my main focus, replacing one obsession with another.

At first, we were like any other couple trying to get pregnant, but after eight months of failed attempts we both knew something was wrong. My first pregnancy was an accident. Why were we experiencing trouble now? Dr. Elliot and I discussed mine and Rob's struggles to conceive. Still, he suggested we try a little longer on our own first. Reluctantly, I agreed; however, by the time we reached the one year mark with no success, I was fit to be tied.

I decided it was time to call and make an appointment. Dr. Elliott ran a few simple tests and determined that I wasn't ovulating regularly. He concluded my grieving affected me in such a way that my body basically shut down, not allowing me to ovulate. With that thought in mind, I wasn't sure how we would correct the problem. I'd always thought a baby would take away the misery I felt, but now my pain was the very thing keeping me from conceiving a child.

Dr. Elliott recommended an exploratory surgery first, to check and make sure all was healthy on the inside. He also offered a few basic suggestions, like taking my temperature and trying an over–the-counter ovulation kit. After my surgery, I started taking an infertility drug to help my body ovulate regularly. I will never forget having that first prescription filled. Hoping this was the answer to our problems, I was certain we would finally get to announce that we were expecting a baby. While it did help get my body back on track, it didn't quite work out like I planned that first month … or the next month … or the next.

And so the infertility process began.

Anyone who has ever experienced the frustration of infertility knows all too well how heart wrenching it can be. You are no longer having sex because you *desire your partner*, but rather to *accomplish a purpose*. Likewise, it is no longer *when you want*, but when *your temperature indicates* it is best. And in the beginning, your husband is more than happy to oblige your constant requests to have sex … just one more time! It's every guy's dream, right? But eventually, even for men, having to perform on command becomes more like a chore than an act of intimacy. Still, you take your temperature each morning before your feet hit the floor, have sex like crazy, run back and forth to all the doctor appointments, and pray your temperature doesn't drop. You hang onto every word your doctor says, hoping he will find a new treatment plan to make this dream you have a reality.

Naturally, you listen to all the well-meaning friends and family who generously offer unsolicited advice and home remedies. You hold your tongue as you listen to countless other women share their struggles with being *too fertile*. Complaining their husbands can't even leave their shoes in the bedroom without them getting pregnant. Nonetheless, as irritating as all the suggestions are at times, if they worked for someone else, you deem them worthy of at least one try. Even if that means standing on your head and maneuvering into all kinds of strange positions to ensure that the sperm would have the best chance possible of reaching the egg. All the while you wonder what's wrong with you and why it comes so easy for the rest of the world. This might sound crazy, but not to those who struggle with infertility. You will go to any and every extreme to conceive a child.

And we did. Nevertheless, month after month, as sure as the sun would rise, my temperature would fall, telling me I wasn't pregnant. Each time it didn't happen, I felt as though I failed. I would have a good cry, pick myself up, and the cycle would begin again...as did Rob's futile attempts to try and console me. I know watching the woman he loved experience disappointment month after month wasn't easy. Thus, our pursuit of a child was one giant emotional roller coaster for both Rob and me.

Eventually, the months turned into years and we witnessed everyone around us having babies while we waited and wondered if it was in God's plan for us. After exhausting all the options a regular OB/GYN can offer, Dr. Elliott suggested we see an infertility specialist, an expert in this field with a better grasp of the next steps we should take.

By this time, I'd become attached to Dr. Elliott and the nurses that worked for him. They were my surrogate family, my life line to the dream Rob and I chased. I had a relationship with them and they knew me by name. Now, he wanted me to go somewhere else. Though I knew he was right, I grieved that loss as well. He gave us the name of a well-respected endocrinologist, and we stepped out in faith to begin a new journey.

Dr. Peter Taliaferro. I could hardly say his name when we first met, but I soon grew to love him and his nurses as much as I did Dr. Elliott's. We started out with all of the usual tests that doctors run on men first. Rob checked out fine…great for him, but not so much for me! It was my body that couldn't sustain the first pregnancy and now we confirmed my body wouldn't allow us to conceive again.

Despite my anxieties, Dr. Taliaferro assured me it was simply a matter of fine tuning things. Changing my medication first, he started me on an injectable drug instead of the oral one Dr. Elliot had prescribed. Of course, with these new medications came new risks, but none at the time that discouraged me from giving them a try. Rob received the honor of giving me the shots I needed every month. Thank goodness that kind of thing never bothered him; I think he even derived some sort of pleasure from it! Still, month after month…shots and more shots…nothing.

However, the idea of throwing in the towel never entered my mind. To me, if I could only get pregnant, I might somehow replace Leighton and ease my pain. That may sound ludicrous since you can't replace a child. But if nothing else, I thought another baby would fill the emptiness losing her had left in my heart. Infertility by itself was an extremely difficult experience to walk through, but coupled with losing Leighton made it almost unbearable.

I am not sure there is a more helpless feeling than to know you are doing all the right things, but in reality you have absolutely no control over the outcome. I read everything I could about what to do and what not to do to get pregnant. After reading what it takes for the sperm and egg to actually connect with each other and form a life, I am surprised anyone conceives. It is truly nothing short of a miracle. And even though medicine has advanced in helping couples like Rob and me, at the end of the day it ultimately rests in the hands of our Creator.

In retrospect, I know now the whole time I hoped a baby would fill the emptiness in my heart, *God wanted to replace that void.* He longed for me to seek Him as hard as I sought this baby. Fixated on my plan, I couldn't see any way possible for me to be happy without Him sending me another child. And as long as I kept trying to find happiness through my own plans, God would allow me to do so.

"Casting all your cares upon Him, for He cares for you."
1 Peter 5:7 (NKJV)

Threads of Healing

With the threads of grief and disappointment wrapped tightly around me, I wasn't sure anything could break their hold, but God works in mysterious ways and His ways are not ours. Who would have thought He would use another baby to help me deal with the loss of my own?

In July of 1993, my sister, Missy, found out she was expecting her first child. Telling my mom and dad right away, she decided to delay another month before telling me. She explained later that she was waiting for the perfect time. Unfortunately, there is never an ideal moment to tell someone who is trying unsuccessfully to conceive a child that you are pregnant, especially if that person is your grieving sister.

Nonetheless, with her beginning to show, she knew telling me was inevitable. She called earlier that morning, informing Rob of her plans to tell me. Missy wanted to allow him some time to prepare for my certain meltdown. After sharing her news with me, we both sat on my sofa in total silence, not knowing what to say to each other. I knew this was an exciting time for her, but I was so disappointed that it wasn't me; I struggled to be happy for her. I couldn't even bring myself to say congratulations. I'd only attended one baby shower since we lost Leighton, but now that my sister was pregnant, I knew not only would I have to attend hers, I would probably be the one giving it… something I wasn't sure I had the strength to do.

By the time of her announcement, Rob and I were at the three-year mark of our struggle to conceive another child and I was emotionally spent. I had very little left to give anyone. As she pulled out of our driveway that afternoon, Rob wrapped his arms around me and held me as I wept. I am ashamed to say, almost the entire time my sister carried her baby, I chose not to acknowledge her pregnancy.

The months flew by and her due date quickly approached, too soon for me and not soon enough for her. Although it wasn't completely obvious, God was working to soften my heart during the last couple of months of her pregnancy. His efforts became apparent to me just a few weeks shy of Missy's due date. During that time, my mom and stepdad were in Canada on vacation. Missy's husband, Chris, was in the Navy and his submarine deployed out to sea. He was scheduled to arrive home in early to mid-February. I couldn't imagine how my sister felt being all alone, and I worried about her that close to delivery.

About that same time, a big snowstorm hit our area. As

usual, the local news covered story after story of pregnant women who couldn't get to the hospital in time to deliver their babies. Concerned that my sister might encounter something like that, Rob and I talked and decided to ask her to come and stay with us. I would never have forgiven myself if she was alone and unable to get to the hospital in time. However, she is strong-willed and independent like me, so assuring us all would be fine, Missy declined our invitation.

I know it probably sounds pathetic, but that simple gesture of reaching out to her was a huge step for me. It felt good to think about someone else for a change and not only myself and my circumstances. My sorrow had consumed me for so long that I didn't take the time to see anyone else's needs. I believe taking my eyes off of myself allowed me to look to God and His plan for me, ultimately breaking down the wall I'd so carefully built. The restoration process was underway!

February 18, 1994, our family gathered at the hospital in anticipation of my niece or nephew's safe arrival. Due to her baby's positioning in the womb, Missy wasn't able to find out the gender prior to the delivery. Throughout her pregnancy, I secretly hoped it would be a boy. After all, it was hard enough watching her and others deliver healthy babies while I waited just to get pregnant. Whenever anyone I knew gave birth to a girl, it intensified the sting that much more. Well, when my brother-in-law walked out and announced I had a niece, my heart sank. Almost four years earlier I lost my daughter, and now my sister was giving birth to a healthy one.

When I became pregnant with Leighton, my sister struggled with thoughts of jealousy, given I was younger and getting married first. My mom encouraged her to never covet anything someone else has, since you never know what their future will bring. Three months later, she wouldn't have traded places with me for anything. Remembering what my mom told her, I stood there and watched them rejoice in their tiny miracle. I didn't know what the future held for my sister or my niece, but I did realize I needed to be happy for them instead of nursing any feelings of envy.

It only took one look at my sister's baby for me to see she was an angel, so delicate and tiny, Alyson was beautiful. Rob and I both fell in love with her and wanted to spend time with her as often as we could. Babysitting Alyson was like playing house or being a grandparent; we got to spoil her and then send her home. I guess it was sort of like therapy for both of us. It is said that time heals all wounds, and to some extent I believe that is true. At the very least, it dulls the pain. But only God can bring complete healing to a hurt this deep. Over the next year, God began to restore my broken heart. I hadn't felt this good since before we lost Leighton.

Likewise, time also has a way of bringing clarity to things. It not only enables us to better understand God's purpose in allowing some of our suffering, it reveals how much we truly trust Him during those tough times. I now realize that how we respond to trials and disappointments greatly affects our future. It can shape us into someone stronger and better if we put our faith and trust in God. Losing Leighton was a defining moment for me. I allowed the sorrow and pain to devour me during those first few years. I put so much effort into my misery; I can honestly tell you there was very little time during those years that my attitude glorified the Lord. And even though my anger and bitterness wasn't bringing Leighton back, it was more important for me to be miserable than to honor God.

I can only imagine how much it hurt God to watch me suffer; after all, He knows first-hand how hard it is to watch your own child die. I believe God wanted desperately to wrap His arms around me and to comfort me, but I *wouldn't* let Him. How could I, when I felt He abandoned me? I didn't see any good in this pain He allowed to enter my life, and I certainly didn't realize *my choices* had played a role in bringing on the suffering I was now encountering.

Regrettably, it took me many years to acknowledge that God did not leave me. He never abandons any of us. But He also never promised Christians a life absent of pain. Rather, He vowed to be there to comfort us during those hard times. If truth be told, for many of us it's not until we find ourselves in the midst of a tragedy that we actually *choose* to seek Him. Really seek Him. During times of pain and suffering we are drawn to Him and strengthened in a way that wouldn't have been possible if not for the hardship. God always has a purpose for everything we endure, even our suffering.

Although I didn't want to believe it, He even had a purpose

in Leighton's death. I know now Leighton never really belonged to us from the start. In fact, Rob and I chose the name Leighton because of its meaning, "belonging to God." I loved the name the first time I heard it, and when she came early it seemed even more appropriate. I didn't truly comprehend the significance until after her death. While Leighton's time here was brief, it was not in vain. It took me years to be able to say this, but I am eternally grateful to the doctors that made an extremely difficult decision the morning Leighton died ... a decision that Rob and I could not make.

Though I longed for my own child, Alyson soon became the instrument God would use to mend my broken heart. How could that be? I wondered. Did God really plan to use my sister's baby to bring my healing to completion?

Indeed, Alyson was an angel sent to heal us all.

"He heals the broken hearted and binds up their wounds."
Psalm 147: 3 (NIV)

Aunt Melme
(Alyson's nickname
for me) and Alyson
Easter Sunday 1995

Alyson, an angel in
disguise

Threads of Rejoicing

Soon after my niece's birth, God began a new work in my heart and the healing I so desperately needed was just around the corner. As I turned to God, He granted my deepest desire. His blessings were more plentiful than I ever imagined.

THE FOLLOWING JANUARY after Alyson was born, I began to pray with a new heart. Of course, I prayed the whole time we tried to conceive, but when there are areas of sin in our lives, God can't and won't honor our prayers. Indeed, He wants to bless us more than we as earthly parents want to bless our children, but we have to be "bless-able."

There are many times now as a parent that I want to do things for my children, but I choose not to, either because of their attitude or because they simply aren't ready to receive it. Sometimes, there are life lessons more valuable for us to learn than receiving the desires of our hearts before we are ready. Like honoring God, regardless of whether He answers our prayers the way we think He should. I wasn't doing that. And even though answering my prayer would have taken away my sadness, I needed to surrender those last threads of bitterness in my heart more than I needed a baby. Coming to this realization was a major turning point for me.

My family continued to be supportive throughout my healing process, each one looking for ways to encourage me... especially, my sister. Right about this same time, Missy was attending Cornerstone Assembly of God. One Sunday morning, a gentleman diagnosed with terminal brain cancer came to give his testimony. He shared an incredible account of healing through the simple act of prayer and fasting. His story so moved my sister that she urged Rob and me to attend a special service they were having later that evening. The experience of fasting was new to me and it aroused my curiosity. I wondered if this might work for us. Praying and trusting God for a miracle, I desperately wanted this to be our breakthrough.

The service began with singing praises to the Lord and my heart was full that night. When they asked anyone praying for a specific need to come forward, Missy led Rob and me down to the front. As we approached the altar, a member of the church greeted us with a warm and caring smile. Following my sister's introduction, he asked, "How can I pray for you tonight?" I explained our struggles to conceive another child after losing our daughter. Resting his hands on my shoulders, he began to pray.

It was an emotional time, but Rob and I both left the

service sure that God heard our cries and would answer them. Everyone in our family agreed to fast one day each week as we continued to pray for a baby. I think we all assumed I would get pregnant that first month; however, I did not. I wouldn't be honest if I didn't say I was disappointed, but I resolved to stay hopeful, hanging on to the promises we claimed that night at my sister's church.

A couple of months later in April, Dr. Taliaferro recommended we give artificial insemination a try. He didn't have to ask me twice; I was willing to give anything a shot. Rob was already giving me shots in my stomach and bottom to increase the number of eggs my body produced. Now, instead of us actually having intercourse, Dr. Taliaferro would take Rob's sperm and release it directly into my uterus with a tiny tube.

We determined the exact day to perform the insemination and again, our family prayed. That morning we raced Rob's specimen over to the lab for processing and then to Dr. Taliaferro's office. The procedure was quick and painless ... it was what came after that was excruciating! Waiting. Though we were used to it, it never became any easier.

Again, I was hopeful this would be the month, but after five years of disappointment I had reservations. As usual, each morning I took my temperature, hoping and praying it wouldn't dip. Usually a dip occurring around day twelve or thirteen after ovulation indicated I should have a cycle in another day or two. Day thirteen rolled around with no dip; day fourteen, fifteen ... still no dip. I wanted so badly to believe

I was pregnant, but I couldn't allow myself to go there, not without a test to confirm it.

The next morning, day sixteen, I was scheduled to work. As soon as I walked through those automatic doors, I went straight down the aisle, grabbed a pregnancy test off the shelf, and raced to the bathroom. In the stall of a grocery store bathroom, I took a pregnancy test. My hands shook and my heart pounded so hard, I was sure the person in the stall beside me could hear. Even after the allotted time passed, I struggled to look down at the stick. Many times over the years I had been late, but not pregnant. What if it was negative again?

Gathering up enough courage, my eyes moved down to see a pink mark inside the tiny box. *It was positive!* Finally, I *was pregnant!* The last time I saw that pink mark was when I discovered I was pregnant with Leighton. My feelings that morning were completely different than the ones I experienced now. Thrilled, I could hardly keep myself from running through the store screaming, "I'm pregnant!" I ran out of the bathroom, up the aisle, and straight to the office to tell my coworker. I honestly don't recall exactly what I said, but I do remember having our own private celebration!

Then, fear and doubt wiggled its way inside my head. I started to wonder, "What if it's wrong? What if it's a false positive?" It happens all the time; I've seen friends who received a *false negative result.* Knowing I couldn't trust just one test, I bought another one and headed back to the bathroom.

By this time, we were at the five-year mark in our battle

to conceive. That's almost sixty months of trying, which also equals sixty months of negative outcomes. It was something I wanted for so long, and in the beginning it seemed obtainable; but, as the years passed, the hope of ever seeing a positive result became more and more remote. No matter what you are waiting for, when the months turn into years, it becomes harder to believe your dream will ever come true.

Despite my fears, the second test was positive, too! It was finally my turn to say, "*I am pregnant!*" May 18, 1995, I was able to announce that I was going to have a baby!

> "Weeping may stay for the night, but rejoicing comes in the morning. Hear, O Lord, and have mercy on me; Lord, be my helper! You have turned for me my mourning into dancing; You have put off my sackcloth and clothed me with gladness."
>
> Psalm 30:5b, 10-11 (NKJV)

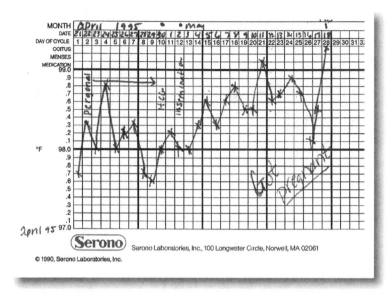

Pregnant at last! My temperature chart April–May 1995

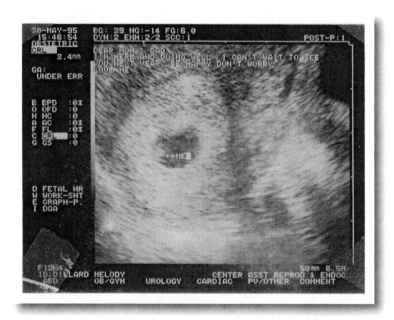

Caleb's heartbeat May 1995

Threads of Love

The Bible likens God's love to that of a mother. As much as I thought I loved Leighton, I would soon experience what real love felt like. From the moment they laid my baby in my arms, my heart has never been the same. This love has only grown deeper and stronger through the years.

THE FIRST CALL I MADE was to Rob, and like me, he struggled to believe the news. Honestly, it seemed like a dream for both of us. Calling Dr. Taliaferro's office next, it was almost as exciting as telling my real family. It thrilled me to inform the nurse I took not one, but two pregnancy tests, and both came back positive! She offered to work me in to have an ultrasound done if I could get off work. Naturally, I broke every speed limit law from the store to the doctor's office. Rob left work and met me there as quickly as he could.

As I lay on the examining table, my eyes fixated on the screen, I could hardly believe it. There was our baby's heartbeat. We'd waited five years for this moment and now it didn't even seem real. Was this really happening, or would I wake up to find it was only a dream? Discovering I was pregnant with this baby was one of the happiest days of my life. At last, an answer to almost six years of prayers!

However, the fear and concern that I may have complications again soon overshadowed our excitement. Having delivered prematurely once, I was now considered a *high risk pregnancy.* Though contemplating that possibility frightened me, the doctors and nurses promised to monitor me closely. We saw a perinatologist, someone who specializes in high risk situations, and he administered ultrasounds that were more sophisticated than the normal kind. Dr. Elliott also kept a close eye on me to make sure there were no signs of preterm labor. Examining my cervix frequently to make sure it stayed closed, he even discussed putting a stitch in, if necessary. We weren't willing to take any risks this time. Leighton came sixteen weeks early, so I focused on getting to the twenty-four week mark safely. Of course, all of this additional care meant a lot more trips to the doctor, but when you're an expectant mother, that's just icing on the cake!

Despite our concerns, aside from a bit of spotting in the first trimester, the pregnancy appeared healthy. Before long, I sported a little baby bump and I couldn't have been happier. Soaking up all the extra attention, I relished every minute of expectant motherhood. Given I have an incurable sweet tooth I also enjoyed the freedom of indulging in quite a few treats over the next nine months! Drinking one chocolate milkshake every morning for breakfast, I also had one before bedtime each night. In fact, I consumed so many Rob joked that my milk may come out chocolate when I finally nursed! Needless to say, along with my baby getting bigger, so was my pant size. In the end I gained a whopping forty pounds, but I didn't mind. I had longed for years to finally feel a baby growing inside of me, so gaining weight was the least of my worries. Life was good and I felt incredibly blessed.

Of course, with all the extra ultrasounds, we were sure to find out the baby's gender. If you are someone who doesn't like to wait, it is one of the most exciting moments for parents-to-be. I remember that day clearly. Naturally, from the start, Rob and I both agreed all we wanted was a healthy baby. But, as for me, I secretly still longed to replace Leighton. Besides, all of my childhood dreams included me as the mother of a little girl. I had big plans of decorating the nursery with soft, pink, girly things and buying frilly dresses with matching hair bows. Never once, in all my dreams, did I imagine myself fixing up a little boy's room. Muddy sneakers, smelly shirts, pockets filled with worms... I simply didn't see myself as the mother of a little boy. Surely it would be a girl, right? I mean, God was listening all this time, wasn't He? I placed an order for a little girl, just like the one I lost.

The morning of the appointment we waited with anticipation; I could hardly contain my excitement. Rehearsing things in my mind, I could almost hear the technician announce, "It's a girl!" Even Rob thought it was going to be a little girl. If my memory serves me right, I had even made a purchase or two for the baby girl I was sure to have. So, you can only imagine the expression on my face when the technician told us he could see "the plumbing." You could have bought me for a nickel.

"You're going to have a baby boy!" he said.

We're going to have a boy? What in the world am I going to do with a little boy? I thought. As we drove home that day, I *was* grateful our baby was healthy, but I wouldn't be honest if I didn't confess his gender left me a little disappointed. I am sure there are moms who can relate to that sentiment and some who will consider it unthinkable for me to have felt that way, much less verbalize it. My thoughts even left me ashamed. Especially after trying for so long, why did I feel anything less than total jubilation?

Let me explain. My mom came from a big family. Between my mom and her nine siblings, there were eleven of us cousins. Ten girls and only *one* boy! Our family simply didn't produce boys and we really didn't know what to do with them! Sounds terrible, I know, but it's the cold hard truth.

Needless to say, now I am forever grateful that while God gives us the freedom to choose some things, He doesn't relinquish total control to us. For on that morning, if given a box to check indicating whether I wanted a boy or girl, I would have marked the space for a girl, ultimately forfeiting one of the greatest honors given to me so far ... the honor of being the mother of a son.

Caleb Grayson, "faithful, brave messenger," entered our

world on January 18, 1996, at 7:26 a.m. He weighed 8 lbs. 4½ oz. and he was 21¼ inches long. Compared to Leighton, he looked like a toddler! From the moment they laid him in my arms, it was love at first sight. And it was equally as exciting for Rob; he was now the proud father of a son. Though we handled Leighton's death differently, we both anticipated this moment for many years. We were officially parents! Embracing my new role as a mother, I took a leave of absence from work and began caring for my child.

Even though Caleb only arrived one week early, I knew by the way he kicked he was chomping at the bit to get here earlier. His strong will and impatient spirit showed through immediately, as I tried to teach him how to nurse. We fought for several days until he finally got the hang of things. His determination continued to grow right along with him, surfacing almost daily in some way. It became even more evident once he was mobile. When Caleb began crawling, he would make his way into our foyer and head straight for the steps, hurriedly trying to climb up while I raced to fetch him. After relocating him, no sooner did I turn my back I would see him crawling in the direction of the steps again. And I can assure you, his relentless nature has only grown with time. To this day, Caleb knows exactly what he wants and he goes to great lengths to ensure he gets it!

After Caleb started talking, like most parents, we had a few things we prompted him to repeat time and time again. One of our favorite questions was, "Caleb, where's Jesus?" Placing his tiny hand over his heart, he would proudly answer, "In my heart." It was totally adorable; we must have asked him that question at least a few hundred times over the years. I am sure he probably thought, "Can't you people remember anything? I just told you ten minutes ago!"

In contrast to his strong will, God blessed Caleb with the biggest, most tender heart you could ever want in a boy. Countless times while growing up, Caleb would come to me confessing something he'd done that was weighing on his conscience, many times sharing things I would never have known if not for his honesty. Along with Caleb's tender heart, he possessed a giant-size faith. Bible Man, a Christian super hero popular during Caleb's childhood, became his role model. Armed with his sword of the spirit and breastplate of righteousness, he ran around the house fighting off evil. Caleb's love and faith in God was always evident to anyone who came in contact with him.

Still, as much as he loved God, his earthly hero was his dad. Caleb wanted to be just like him! I lost count of how many laps he made around the front yard following Rob with his Little Tikes lawn mower. They spent hours wrestling in the great room floor and threw the baseball in the back yard until the mosquitoes brought them inside. Rob, winded and out of breath, ran down the street behind Caleb as he taught him how to ride his first bike. At last, Rob had the huntin' and fishin' buddy every father who loves the outdoors dreams of!

As for me, it would suffice to say my heart hasn't been the

same since the day he entered this world. While Caleb was growing up, I would often ask if he was my *little man*, and he would answer enthusiastically, "Yes, mommy, and you're my *sweet girl*." More times than I can remember, he even made me promise to marry him one day. So although I never dreamed of having a son, I would have to say Caleb is one of the sweetest things God has ever done for me.

In fact, it is actually like receiving a present that you yourself would never have picked. It's something you didn't think you needed, and certainly didn't imagine you would even enjoy. But, to your amazement, with every day that passes, you can't believe how much you love this gift. You don't understand how you managed to survive all those years without it, and now you can't imagine living even one minute without this precious gift.

Recognizing this, I have to wonder how many blessings we miss because we think we know more than God. How often, in those times that we are given a choice, do we opt for what we want and not God's best? All I can say now is, "Thank you, God! Thank you for knowing what I really needed more than I did. Thank you for editing my dream and making it better than I could have ever imagined."

While Caleb brought immeasurable joy to our world and our hearts were full... still something was missing. We weren't complete. I wasn't quite ready to relinquish my dream of having a little girl; and, whether I ever had a little girl or not, I always knew I wanted more than one child. I couldn't imagine Caleb without a brother or sister. Since we experienced so much trouble getting pregnant this time, we chose not to use any birth control after Caleb was born. After all, we were only successful at conceiving two babies in five years. With that in mind, we decided to enjoy our son and see what God had in store for us next.

> "For this child I prayed, and the Lord had granted me my petition which I asked of Him."   1 Samuel 1:27 (NKJV)

*August 1995 — I was
five months pregnant
with Caleb*

*The night we
brought Caleb home
from the hospital
January 19, 1996*

Melody and Caleb 1996

Rob and Caleb—
fishin' buddies

Caleb as Bible Man
Halloween night

Melody and Caleb,
Nags Head summer 1998

Caleb....finally, someone
to hunt with!

Threads of Surrender

Complete and total surrender, while painful, is also a beautiful place. I struggled over the years to surrender my will to anyone or anything, mainly because I always think my plan is better. Faced with more difficulties trying to conceive, God placed someone in my life to help weave in this essential thread.

YEARS PASSED. Caleb grew, and so did my desire to have another child. By the time he turned two, I had started dabbling with some interior design work. At first, I was faux finishing furniture for a small home décor shop, but it quickly turned into a thriving decorating business. It kept me busy and took my mind off of the fact that I wasn't pregnant. However, with Caleb's fourth birthday approaching, I could hear my biological clock ticking. Even Caleb realized that he didn't have a brother or sister yet. While we were waiting in the checkout line at Wal-Mart one afternoon, the cashier asked him if he had any siblings. Looking at her as seriously as a three-year-old could, he said, "No ma'am, but I'm praying for one!" And pray he did.

Well, I figured if he was going to do his part, I needed to do mine, too. Abandoning our plan to conceive naturally, back to the drawing board we went. With one quick phone call we made an appointment to go back in to see Dr. Taliaferro. Rob and I knew the drill. After all, it's not really a routine you ever forget. I immediately began taking my temperature again and Rob started injecting me with high doses of infertility drugs. Why waste time, I thought; we'll do all the same things we did to get pregnant with Caleb and we'll end up with the same result, right? Wrong!

First month, negative...second month, negative...third, fourth, fifth month and still no baby. I knew in my heart there was a problem. I didn't know what, but something was different this time.

At first, I racked my brain to come up with an answer. We were using all the same medications and I stayed on top of taking my temperature. What was wrong? Along with my strong will, I am also an obsessive thinker. I have an insatiable desire to know the reason why things do or do not happen. So needless to say, I was totally obsessing by this time! Despite how much I contemplated things, nothing made sense to me. I did recall a few instances where some mistakes were made. We actually went in to be inseminated twice, only to discover I had already ovulated. That kind of error doesn't usually happen when the doctor is monitoring things so closely. There are ultrasounds and exams, checking and double-checking to track where your body is in its cycle. How could that happen?

If we were being that careful and scrutinizing everything, why were we making these blunders?

After a few more months the answer finally came to me when one of my friends announced that she was pregnant. Like me, she had been trying for quite some time and soon after learning she was expecting the doctors discovered a serious complication. When I heard about her situation, I wondered if I might encounter problems if I were pregnant, too. Maybe that was the reason God wasn't allowing us to conceive. Perhaps He knew something I didn't. As I stood in the shower one morning, the thought came to me. "You're not trusting God completely, Melody." The realization was a tough one and even though I couldn't explain what I was feeling, I knew in my heart we needed to stop the treatments. It was time to let go and surrender it to The Lord.

Sounds simple enough, right? Not normally, but in that instance, I found it effortless. To this day I can't explain what came over me. It was truly nothing short of a miracle....and when I say miracle, it ranks right up there with the parting of the Red Sea. I even remember joking with one of my friends, telling her if Mary conceived baby Jesus without a husband, then this shouldn't be any problem if God wanted us to have another child! I had such a deep settled peace, I was certain it was God.

From that moment, Rob and I relinquished control and I began praying, "Lord, I trust you. If I never get pregnant again, I trust that You know something I don't." I'm still not sure why those particular words came to me, but they did. Normally my prayers sound more like this, "Lord, I trust You as long as Your plan matches up with mine." Or, "I know You might have a plan Lord, but I really need you to do A, B, and C in order for me to be happy." But for some reason, this time I trusted Him to do His will without my interference.

As fall approached, so did the beginning of a new phase in parenthood for Rob and me. Caleb started preschool! Rob and I decided to send him to a Christian school in hopes of continuing there through his elementary years. We were blessed with an amazing woman as his teacher, Della Meccariello. Her gentle and humble spirit was a sweet aroma of Christ. Just as beautiful on the inside as she was on the outside, Della was the kind of person you are drawn to. I wanted to linger in her presence, hoping some of what she had would miraculously rub off on me. We all loved her, but Caleb took a special liking to Mrs. Meccariello from the moment he met her. She actually became the *first other woman* in his life. In fact, on the ride home from school one afternoon, he happily announced that they were getting married one day and naming all their children Buzz Lightyear! Of course, she was thrilled when I shared the news with her!

Those first few weeks went quickly and Caleb adjusted to his new routine. Everything seemed to be going great... until September 29th. Only one month into the school year, tragedy struck Della's family. Her oldest son, Tanner, decided to go for a ride with some friends one afternoon. Minutes later, a mere few hundred feet outside the subdivision where they lived, there was an accident. The young boy driving that day had been drinking. Driving too fast, he lost control of the SUV they were in and hit a tree head on: three boys, three girls, and one tree. The driver walked away from the accident, but not all the other kids were as fortunate. Della's son was one of the three that died that afternoon.

As I watched the evening news, phone calls from other parents with pieces of the story began rolling in. I'd only known Della a month, but I already loved her. My heart broke as I knew from losing Leighton a small part of the pain they were about to endure. Three families and countless lives, changed forever. The entire school and community mourned.

Tanner's family decided to hold the funeral in the school sanctuary where Della taught and attended church. In preparation for the services, someone called and asked if I would help monitor the hallways that morning. They didn't want the students trying to sneak out of the classrooms during the funeral. I thought it was a good idea, and naturally I wanted to be there to support Della, so I agreed.

Heartbroken family and friends filled the sanctuary. We joined the praise team in singing some of Tanner's favorite songs and friends shared stories in remembrance of Tanner; there wasn't a dry eye to be found. Normally I am not much of a *crier*, but that morning I stood in the back of the sanctuary sobbing inconsolably. Reminiscing over Leighton and her funeral, I relived the pain of her death. All the emotions I'd felt when we lost her suddenly came rushing back. As I stood there steeping in my own grief, I saw Della stand to her feet and raise her hands in a motion of praise.

How could she do that? I wondered. Praising God during the most painful time of her life? Many times over the years, I listened to the words of the song "We Bring the Sacrifice of Praise." Now, I was actually witnessing someone do just that. It was, without a doubt, the most selfless act I have ever been privileged to see. It was a life changing moment for me...a defining one. I looked around the room that morning and wondered how anyone could walk away unchanged.

Overcome with emotion, I no longer knew if my tears were because of the pain and hurt I knew she was experiencing, or because of her offering to God. Watching her, I realized it wasn't that Della loved her son any less than I loved Leighton, or that she hurt any less than I hurt; it was that she loved God more than I did. My mind went back to how I handled Leighton's death. I knew at the time I didn't walk through that trial honoring God. Della's sacrifice showed me what true surrender looked like. My being there was no coincidence...God was preparing me for something.

Not wanting to leave the sanctuary, I stood in the back and quietly soaked in the moment. Talking with God, I told Him over and over again, "I want to be like her. I want to praise You even when my circumstances don't make sense, or when I am hurt and disappointed. Regardless of what is going on in my life, I want to praise You simply because You are good and You deserve it." As the service concluded, I couldn't erase the image of Della standing there praising God.

It was very surreal to watch her choose to do something that took every ounce of strength she could muster, simply because she knew it would glorify God. Della later shared with me that at the moment she lifted her hands into the air, her arms felt as if there were hundred- pound weights restraining them. She also confessed standing to her feet was the only way she knew to come against Satan, worrying if she didn't do it at that moment, she wasn't sure she would. At the time, and even now, I find it hard to relinquish my will to God regarding things that are much smaller than what she went through that day. That morning, Della chose to honor God in the midst of a tragedy that would have turned many away from Him.

Still, her surrendering to God wasn't a one-time thing. It took time for her to come back to school, and when she did nothing about her attitude changed. Just as she modeled Christ-like character at Tanner's funeral, she did so once she returned. Each day she came clothed in humility and grace. Her strength came from a place that is only obtainable when you walk hand in hand with God. When I looked at her, I could see the pain in her eyes, and yet she exemplified the love of Christ. I knew the Lord carried her, for in her own strength it wasn't possible.

It is said that you can tell a lot about a person by the way they handle trials and disappointments. I think there is an abundance of truth in that statement. After all, it's not until we are squeezed that we see what we are really made of. The first time Rob and I were squeezed, what came out of me wasn't so great. Choosing not to trust God, instead I wrapped myself up in my grief. After watching Della, I knew I wanted to do things differently the next time I faced a trial. I wanted God to look down on me and be proud of how I handled a difficult circumstance. Her example taught me how to surrender my will to God, including my struggles to conceive another child. If another baby wasn't in God's plans for me, then I wanted to accept it and praise Him the way Della did.

I would soon discover that there was a reason God wasn't answering my prayer in my time. He simply wanted to save my life.

> "Trust in the Lord with all your heart and lean not on your own understanding; in all your ways submit to Him and He will make your paths straight."
>
> Proverbs 3:5-6 (NIV)

Della Meccariello and Caleb at his
preschool graduation May 2001

Threads of Trust

Cancer. The Big C. Something everyone fears, that touches so many lives in one way or another. Pregnant. A word I longed to hear many times over the years. Both sounded hard to believe, but hearing them together seemed unimaginable. After witnessing Della's sacrifice of praise during her son's funeral, I vowed to walk through this trial differently than I had all the others. As I chose to trust God, He strengthened my resolve each and every day.

WITH DELLA'S EXAMPLE of total surrender fresh in my mind, I placed my desire of having another baby in God's hands. October and November flew by, and soon we were celebrating Christmas and Caleb's 5th birthday. And, in spite of my upcoming surgery, all in our world appeared perfect.

That is until the morning of January 22, 2001.

Leaving the hospital with a diagnosis of cancer and what appeared to be an untimely pregnancy, we had many things to consider. The ride home that morning was long and quiet;

I don't think Rob or I had any words to express our emotions. I couldn't help but wonder if all the infertility treatments were the cause of this. With no family history of cancer and just finishing up eight months of injections, it was the only explanation that made any sense. I knew from the start the danger associated with taking the drugs. Still, after weighing the advantages against the disadvantages, I concluded the idea of never being a mother was more emotionally painful than any physical problem I might incur. Now, I wondered if this cancer could be the result of taking all the different medications. Even if that was the case, I had no regrets, at least not with that decision.

The only remorse I was encountering concerned our intimacy before marriage. Many years earlier, I'd acknowledged that this decision brought about so much of our pain and suffering. And Dr. Elliott confirmed my grief over losing Leighton was the reason my body shut down, forcing me to seek infertility treatments in the first place. If all this was true, then my choices as a young woman had altered my tapestry more than I imagined possible.

While I pondered this, I replayed Dr. Truitt's recommendation to terminate this pregnancy. How was it possible we faced the same decision again? Granted, eleven years earlier our reasons were different, but if I struggled with it then, how could I possibly make this choice now...as a mother. Why would God allow this to happen? As much as I tried to make sense of it, I couldn't.

Rob and I pulled into our driveway, and I desperately longed to close my eyes and fall asleep. Maybe I would wake up to find that it was only a bad dream. Still sluggish from the anesthesia, I made my way upstairs and crawled into bed. It wasn't my body that needed the rest as much as my mind. Even so, I struggled to quiet my thoughts as I curled up into my usual fetal position and cried myself to sleep.

My mom stayed to help Rob make all the necessary phone calls and receive the ones steadily coming in. Once everything settled down, she mustered up enough nerve to call my dad. A phone call no one wanted to make. He was driving home from a trip in the Mid-West that morning and was unaware of the report we had received. I have always been very close to my dad and I knew hearing this news wasn't going to be easy, especially since he was alone and so far from home. Driving 1000 miles across the country is a long drive anyway, but when all you want to do is hold your child, it feels even farther. My mom tried to comfort my dad as best she could, but as a frightened mother, she wasn't really in a frame of mind to console anyone. When my dad finally spoke with Rob, he wept as he thanked him for finding the lump. He understood that, despite the gravity of the situation, the early detection of the cancer raised my chances of survival.

It wasn't long before Rob's mom arrived home with Caleb. Rather than accompanying us to the hospital that morning, she had offered to get him ready for school and pick him up that afternoon. Rob had already updated her about the cancer diagnosis and the baby; like everyone else, she was completely blindsided. After talking with my mom and Rob, Sandy came upstairs to see me. She knocked on the bedroom door and quietly came in to wake me. We hugged each other and she offered some words of encouragement before we made our way downstairs. By this time, friends started to trickle in, each one offering to lend a helping hand.

One of our first visitors was Jerome Hancock, our pastor. The week before, I had talked with him and mentioned my surgery. At the time, I had asked him to pray and assured him it was nothing to be concerned about. But now that we faced something more serious, he wanted to spend time in prayer with Rob and me. While he couldn't offer any answers as to why God would allow this to happen, his presence was comforting. He assured Rob and me both that he supported us in whatever decision we made regarding the pregnancy. Confused and distraught, at that point I honestly had no idea what to do. Should I listen to Dr. Truitt and terminate? I understood the importance of considering Caleb and the possibility I might leave him without a mother, but what about this baby?

Heading back to Dr. Truitt' office, Rob and I were still in shock and trying to process the news. Cancer and a baby; we never entertained either diagnosis prior to that morning, at least not seriously. After meeting with Dr. Truitt and talking things over again, she made it clear she wasn't budging on her recommendation, again emphasizing she believed there was more cancer left in the remaining breast tissue. She told Rob and me, "The best course of treatment is to terminate the pregnancy, have a radical mastectomy, and proceed with aggressive treatment." Listening to her words, I felt helpless, just as I did the day Leighton was born. I searched for questions to ask that might cause her to respond differently, but there were none. On the outside she presented a strong façade, as if it was easy to recommend we choose to take the life of our baby.

When I realized she wasn't going to change her mind from a medical standpoint, I decided to take a different approach, asking her, "Do you believe in miracles?"

Still unwilling to give, she answered, "No."

And I, unwilling to retreat, firmly responded, "Well, I do! And I think God is more than capable of taking care of this baby and me." I am not sure if I truly believed the words that came out of my mouth at that exact moment, but I knew I needed to say them. Voicing them out loud gave me a certain amount of strength.

While Dr. Truitt showed little emotion when delivering this news to Rob and me that day, I am sure it must have been difficult. After all, telling another mother that in order to save her own life she would have to take the life of her child couldn't have been easy. Her initial recommendation to remove the mass had indeed saved my life, and as much as I respected her for that, I wasn't sure I could agree with her on this next step. We left her office that day certain of only one thing.....she wasn't the doctor for us.

Rob and I arrived back home to a house full of loved ones

waiting to wrap their arms around us. Our phone continued ringing with family and friends offering love and support. Everyone called their churches and small groups to place our names on the different prayer lists. The outpouring of love was mind-boggling.

Once again recalling Della's sacrifice of praise, I immediately made the choice to react to this struggle differently than the way I responded to Leighton's death. Having spent a great deal of time asking God why we lost Leighton, I vowed not to ask that question this time. *I was going to choose to honor God.* After all, would I have felt any better if it was my sister or a friend diagnosed with this cancer? So many times over the years when I faced a trail I asked God "why me?" Shouldn't the question really be "why not me?"

Over the next couple of days, I began to mentally sort through the events that had transpired. As I did, I was astonished how all the pieces fit together…like a puzzle. During those last few months leading up to my diagnosis, I prayed, "God, I trust you. If I never get pregnant again, I trust that you know something I don't." *And He did.* God sees the final tapestry of our lives before we are even born. Therefore, He knew I only had one month where I could safely conceive a child. So, all the months that I felt my prayers were going unanswered, He was actually working to save my life. He was waiting for Rob to find the lump. Throughout all of the infertility mishaps, when I ovulated early and wondered why, God was in control.

Romans 8:28 tells us, "And we know that all things work

together for good to those who love God, to those who are called according to His purpose." Not only did God know I had a limited time frame where I could safely conceive, He actually orchestrated this baby's conception on the very night that Rob found the lump in my breast. And that's not all. January 22nd, the day of my diagnosis, is the anniversary date for the decision of Roe vs. Wade, legalizing abortion. How amazing is that? Our God is such a God of details, He cares about every facet of our lives. I honestly believe He planned this whole incident to occur on that date, for the "wow" factor if nothing else!

I will admit it took me a couple of days to come to terms with it all, but the perfection of God's timing could not have been clearer. The doctors even told me that if I had conceived before we discovered the lump the cancer more than likely would have gone undiagnosed. With all the changes that take place in a woman's breasts after she gets pregnant, it would have been hard to find the mass. Once I realized this, I wasn't sure how God would take care of things, I just knew He would.

I'd already surrendered my desires to have another baby to God, believing that He would fulfill His plan in His time. Now, with medical professionals telling me to think about myself and my child at home, I had a new set of challenges before me. Dr. Elliott, my OB/GYN, shared the same opinion as Dr. Truitt. I should terminate the pregnancy to increase my chances of survival. That was especially hard to hear considering he was the one who helped us through all those years of infertility. With that in mind, Rob and I decided to get a second opinion. Surely we could find someone who would say it was feasible to carry the baby and take the chemotherapy needed to help me; or, maybe we could delay the treatments until after the baby's birth. There had to be another option. I was determined to figure out a solution, a different formula, so that things would work out and we could keep this baby.

I immediately called the Massey Cancer Center at MCV in Richmond, Virginia, and made an appointment with one of the head surgeons in the breast cancer center. We heard wonderful things about Dr. Brent and I hoped he would have the answers we were searching for. After we explained the situation to his nurse, she made room for us in the appointment book. She also requested Dr. Bain, one of the head oncologists, sit in on the meeting. Rob and I asked our pastor to accompany our family the morning of the appointment...not that he knew any more than we did, but to support us in this life and death decision.

Still, after going over all the details of my case carefully—it didn't matter how we presented it—Dr. Brent said it simply wouldn't work. He, too, agreed with Dr. Truitt and Dr. Elliott. In a polite but firm way, Dr. Brent told us, "People simply don't choose to do what you are asking us to let you do." I asked him every way I could think of to keep the baby and get the help necessary to save my life, but he stood firm: terminate the pregnancy and proceed with aggressive treatment. With this final recommendation, he gave us absolutely no hope. The examining room where we met that day was relatively small in size.

With our pastor and some family members present, it made for close quarters. Pastor Hancock later described he felt as though the walls were closing in around us, making the room seem that much smaller.

Needless to say, we left the meeting discouraged and defeated. But as we walked down the hallway recapping everything, something rose up inside me. Something that said, We can do this! God can do this! Rob and I hadn't conceived a baby on our own in eleven years, so for me to get pregnant without medical intervention was truly a miracle. If God could perform that miracle, I knew He must have a plan. It was almost like someone flipped a light switch in me.

Suddenly, my biggest fear wasn't the cancer. Instead, I worried that I might not have the courage to trust God. I was concerned that I might take the doctor's advice and not keep the baby. As we stood there talking, I voiced my thoughts to Rob and our pastor.

What if this is a testimony in the making? What if God wants to orchestrate something really big here and I get in His way because I won't trust Him? I questioned.

Thinking about my situation, I realized there are probably millions of *unborn testimonies* simply because we lack the faith to completely trust in God. I knew this was far bigger than Rob and me. And even though there were still many uncertainties, I didn't want to miss the opportunity to be a part of God's amazing plan. So, as my son says, "Go big, or go home."

Once we took our eyes off our circumstances, it was easy

to see God's handprint everywhere. With each day that passed, the thought of making a choice concerning the baby slowly disappeared. The only decision we had to make was whether we would surrender and trust God.

We chose to trust God!

> "When I am afraid, I put my trust in you. In God, whose word I praise, in God I trust and am not afraid. What can mere mortals do to me?"
>
> Psalm 56:3-4 (NIV)

Threads of Provision

After resolving to trust in God, I soon realized His provision at every turn. He provided the doctors and treatments that would allow me to fight this cancer while keeping our baby healthy, as well as family and friends who were with us each step of the way. God's goodness knew no boundaries.

THOUGH IT SEEMED HOPELESS with more than one doctor telling us we needed to terminate the pregnancy, God provided the answers to our problem before we even knew it existed. In December of 2000, a month before we discovered the lump, my sister attended an Emmaus Walk, a spiritual retreat. While there, she met Joe Anderson, a pastor from the Richmond area. He shared that his church held a weekly healing service where people saw God move in miraculous ways. I know what you're thinking. There are always negative connotations that go along with saying "healing service." But I absolutely believe that God does work through prayer and He uses certain people to bring about physical healing. Pastor Joe has an incredible testimony and a special anointing on his life. God used him, and continues to use him, in a mighty way.

Just as when Rob and I attempted to conceive a baby, we turned to God for a miracle. Shortly after the biopsy, we attended one of Pastor Joe's healing services. Arriving with our posse of friends and family, we filled an entire pew and a half. From the moment this journey began, support is one thing we never lacked. If there is any truth to there being power in numbers, we had it covered.

The service began with a time of praise and worship, and the presence of the Holy Spirit filled the sanctuary. The longer I sat, the more anxious I became ... not in a bad way, but excited to see what God would do. Finally, Pastor Joe invited those who needed physical healing to make their way down to the front.

Naturally, I couldn't get out of the pew fast enough! As Rob and I walked down the aisle, a peace came over me and my anxiousness slowly disappeared. After explaining our situation to Pastor Joe, he asked Rob to place his hand on the spot where the mass was before the biopsy. From the instant Pastor Joe began to pray, I started to feel a dull pain, a feeling I hadn't noticed prior to that moment. Praying for several minutes, he then asked me to move down front to allow others to agree with him in prayer. I made my way towards the altar and several of the elders gathered around me to pray and claim my healing. It was a powerful experience, unlike anything I have ever encountered.

Lying in bed later that night, I began to sense a vibrating

sensation in the exact spot where Rob's hand rested during Pastor Joe's prayer. It felt as though someone put a cell phone set on vibrate mode to my side. Continuing intermittently throughout the night, it was the strangest thing I had ever felt. In fact, it was so strong that it woke me up several times. Stopping as suddenly as it started, I never experienced the pain or vibrations after that night. There is no doubt in my mind that God touched my body during that service.

And that was just the beginning of His bringing perfect order to an otherwise chaotic time, starting with showing us the doctors who would come up with the perfect treatment plan for us. Dr. Bain, the oncologist who sat in on the meeting with Dr. Brent, contacted me to say he thought there was a way to continue the pregnancy and still take the chemotherapy. He explained as long as we waited until after the first trimester, everything should be fine. Once I passed the first twelve weeks, the baby would already be fully formed: arms, legs, and all the internal organs. From that point forward, he or she would simply continue to mature and grow.

This was the first good news since hearing the diagnosis. As relieved as I was, it gave me pause that he told me I could have chemotherapy while pregnant. How can doctors caution pregnant women about taking over-the-counter medications when pregnant, yet allow me to go through chemotherapy? Dr. Bain clarified that some drugs can penetrate the placental wall while others aren't able to do so. Meeting that criterion, doctors consider chemotherapy safe during pregnancy.

Since Dr. Elliott wasn't on the same page with us keeping the baby, we decided to consult with a different OB/GYN. A female friend at work gave Rob the name of another doctor, Dr. Williams. I couldn't imagine seeing anyone other than Dr. Elliott, and I dreaded the thought of starting over with a new gynecologist. With so many things changing in my world during this time, I needed at least one constant; it appeared as if that wasn't an option.

However, after meeting with Dr. Williams, I was pleasantly surprised how comfortable he made me feel. He was relaxed enough to put me at ease, yet cautious enough to let me know I was in good hands. Even though I was his first pregnant patient with cancer, I felt confident in his abilities. I attributed that largely to his incredible sense of humor and phenomenal bedside manner. A positive relationship between a pregnant woman and her gynecologist is so important in her prenatal experience, especially when the pregnant woman has cancer. God's provision in this area was incredible!

And He didn't skimp with the breast surgeon either. Dr. Truitt performed the biopsy, but now that we faced a more serious surgery, I wanted someone with years of experience. I needed a doctor who had performed this procedure successfully many times, without any complications. Although I knew Dr. Truitt was more than competent, her age indicated she didn't have the kind of skill I desired.

Praying and asking God for a confirmation on which surgeon to use, I received a phone call one afternoon from a woman who heard about our situation. After I talked with her for several minutes, she said, "You need to meet with Dr. Geoffery Caldwell. He is the best in his field." When I heard her say his name, I couldn't believe it. That was exactly who we wanted to perform the initial biopsy, and here a stranger was bringing him up again. With that in mind, I decided to call Dr. Caldwell's office and see if anything had changed. *Miraculously,* he had an opening and could meet with us for a consultation. Just a couple of weeks earlier, he was booked solid for six weeks. I sensed a total confirmation from the Lord that he was the right surgeon.

Within minutes of meeting Dr. Caldwell, I was even more secure in our decision. While he was small in stature, there was nothing little about his personality, especially his million dollar smile! It could brighten the darkest situation and his positive attitude was precisely what I needed. I've already explained how important bedside manner is to me. Well, I really needed to have that *warm, fuzzy feeling* with this doctor; especially since he was the one who might be removing my breast!

Originally, Dr. Truitt recommended a radical mastectomy, but Dr. Caldwell gave me the option of having a lumpectomy. After weighing the advantages and disadvantages, I decided to go with Dr. Truitt' suggestion and have a complete mastectomy. Considering I wasn't very well endowed, I chose not to let that little bit of fluff keep me from living a long healthy life. Besides, the way I saw it, this was my chance to get a new pair of breasts ... I certainly wasn't going to pass that up!

Bringing Dr. Caldwell up to speed with Dr. Bain's plan, we found he was totally on board; at last, we could see we had the right team working together for us. Everyone agreed I would have the mastectomy and wait until after my first trimester to begin chemotherapy.

We scheduled the surgery for February 7th, totally at peace that God was in control.

> "Therefore I tell you, do not worry about your life, what you will eat or drink; or about your body, what you will wear. Is not life more than food and the body more than clothes? Look at the birds of the air; they do not sow or reap or store away in barns, and yet your heavenly Father feeds them. Are you not much more valuable than they? Can any one of you by worrying add a single hour to your life?"
>
> Matthew 6:25-27 (NIV)

Threads of Petition

Even though God freely offered His provision, we prayed. Throughout the entire process, we continually submitted ourselves to the Lord in prayer. Night and day, we knew there were hundreds, if not thousands, of people praying for us and the life of our child. What could be greater than knowing so many people rooted for us this way?

WEDNESDAY FEBRUARY 7TH, 2001, arrived sooner than I anticipated. The night before, phone calls from family and friends inundated us as they sent their love and prayers. It meant so much, but as the night went on I longed for peace and quiet. I needed some time for Rob and me to digest the events of the next day. I am not sure, even now, how one processes the fact that you have cancer, but I needed to at least try.

I wasn't really scared of losing my breast; that part was never in the forefront of my mind. Even when Dr. Caldwell presented the option of choosing a lumpectomy, I gave it very little consideration. It just didn't make sense not to be as aggressive as possible when I weighed all the facts: my age, the chance of recurrence, and the aggressiveness of the cancer. What good would it be to keep my breast and lose my life? I never felt like they defined me as a woman, anyway. I am not sure if that was a provision that God made for me or not, but I was, and am, still thankful for that.

On the morning of my surgery, walking through the doors of the hospital again was surreal. Dr. Caldwell carefully went over everything with Rob and me in the days leading up to the surgery to ensure we knew what to expect. Once again, we arrived with our own entourage of family and close friends. I am not so sure Rob was all that crazy about the *hen party* that suddenly erupted, but I was glad they were there. The men who walk beside a woman going through breast cancer need support too, even if they don't want to admit it.

Unsure of what the day would hold my family huddled together in the waiting room of St. Mary's Hospital. There is something to be said for what happens inside the walls of a hospital waiting room. Loved ones come to support each other, stories are told, and relationships forged that might not have happened except for the unfortunate circumstances people find themselves in. My family did what many other families confronted with a crisis do ... they began to pray. They prayed with little or no regard to the strangers who might overhear their pleas to the Lord.

Yet even as we prayed that morning there was a different atmosphere from just sixteen short days ago. With the biopsy,

I truly wasn't worried that it would be cancer. The doctors had assured us the lump was more than likely benign. Knowing that, there weren't really any uncertainties going into the operating room, at least not in my mind. However, this time while we trusted God, there were still unanswered questions looming. Was there any cancer in the lymph nodes? Had it spread to any other organs? What stage was it? Now, we waited to see whether the healing we desperately sought was a reality or if the surgery would confirm Dr. Truitt' initial suspicions of cancer throughout the entire breast tissue.

Finally, the nurse came for me. It was time to go back so they could begin prepping me for the mastectomy. I said my goodbyes and walked away a little nervous, but certain I was covered in prayer. Within a couple of hours Dr. Caldwell returned, assuring Rob the surgery went well and that he would be allowed to see me in recovery soon. He explained he'd removed ten lymph nodes, one being the sentinel node. The sentinel node is the first lymph node to which cancer cells are most likely to spread from a primary tumor. This would be a significant factor in determining whether the cancer, in fact, spread beyond my breast. Preparing Rob, Dr. Caldwell added, "It usually takes about a week to get the biopsy report back."

As adults, we no longer view a week in the same way we did when we were a child. With our lives moving at such a fast pace, we tend to regard a week as a relatively short span of time. That is, unless you are waiting to find out if cancer has reached any of your other organs. Then a week suddenly feels like an eternity again.

So once more we prayed. We actually took it a step further and asked God for a "fleece." During Old Testament times, when people would pray and ask God for things, they would request a tangible response. For example, in the book of Judges, Gideon asked God for a fleece, or sign, to indicate that God was with him. In this particular story, Gideon says to God,

"'If you will save Israel by my hands as you have promised—look, I will place a wool fleece on the threshing floor. If there is dew only on the fleece and all the ground is dry, then I will know that you will save Israel by my hand.' And that is exactly what happened. Gideon rose early the next day; he squeezed the fleece, and wrung out the dew—a bowlful of water. Then Gideon said to God, 'Do not be angry with me, but let me speak just once more: let it now be dry only on the fleece, but on all the ground let there be dew.' And God did so that night. It was dry on the fleece only, but there was dew on all the ground" (Judges 6:36-40).

Praying, we asked God to give priority to my lab work and speed the process along. We also asked Him to let the biopsy report show no cancer in the lymph nodes, as well as the remaining breast tissue. If this was the case, then that would be our sign that it would be okay for us to continue the pregnancy. My sister especially stood strong the entire time that we needed to believe God's report and not man's.

Thus, we all united in the same prayer and lifted it up before the throne room of heaven ... and waited.

> "Do not be anxious about anything, but in every situation, by prayer and petition, with thanksgiving, present your request to God. And the peace of God, which transcends all understanding, will guard you hearts and your minds in Christ Jesus."
>
> Philippians 4: 6-7 (NIV)

Threads of Blessings

Threads of blessings appeared continuously during my battle with cancer and my pregnancy. One of those fortunate ones who breezed through everything, I even had to remind myself that I had cancer at all. I can honestly tell you that focusing on all the good things I had rather than all the bad actually made the trial one of the sweetest times of my life.

Even as we waited for God to answer our prayers regarding the test results, He took care of me. Indeed, before, during, and after the surgery, God's protection blessed us. The nurses made me as comfortable as possible during my hospital stay and surprisingly, I felt pretty good. Other than the fact that the drain tube was a complete nuisance, I only encountered a small amount of tenderness around the surgical site. I'm not sure if that was due to my high tolerance to pain or the medication they administered into my IV. Either way, it wasn't nearly as bad as I expected, especially considering the fact they removed my entire left breast!

Bandages now covered that side of my body, and even

though I couldn't see anything, I knew that I no longer had *a pair of breasts*. Just hours before, I gave little thought to that fact, yet acknowledging it did feel a little strange. I was glad the biopsy and mastectomy occurred within a couple weeks of each other; it offered little time to browse the internet in search for images of what my body would look like after having this kind of procedure... probably a good thing, or should I say a *God* thing. Even though I was at peace with my decision, I still struggled with a certain amount of fear and trepidation about seeing myself for the first time. Knowing all the reconstructive surgeries would have to wait until after the baby came, I assured myself that whatever I looked like now, it was temporary.

At the moment, I was more concerned with lasting complications than my outward appearance. Several people had warned me about potential side effects that can occur when having a mastectomy, like not being able to raise my arm or having a permanently swollen arm afterwards. These were some of the specific reasons I wanted Dr. Caldwell to perform the surgery. With his expertise, I put these concerns to rest, and I could raise my arm straight up over my head within a few hours of recovery. One of the other problems associated with a mastectomy is a condition called Lymphedema. This can develop when the lymph nodes are damaged or impaired. Again, all was perfect! And as for the test results taking a week or more... not on God's watch! Not only did we receive the biopsy report in two days, but we got a completely clear report. No cancer in any of the lymph nodes or remaining breast tissue! This is where we all took a deep breath and offered up *great big thanks!*

My mom stayed at the hospital with me, while Sandy helped Rob at home with Caleb. The cancer diagnosis completely turned our life upside down in the blink of an eye. Only two weeks earlier, my days were filled with a to-do list a mile long, usually consisting of more things than are possible to accomplish in a week. I ran from one activity to another, squeezing in the errands and chores, sure the world would stop if I didn't check them off. Suddenly, I had a new perspective. None of those vitally important things seemed so essential anymore. And not just for me. My family's schedule miraculously cleared, and they were available to help Rob and me at a moment's notice. For once, everyone was at my beck and call! And I only had to get pregnant and have cancer to command this attention!

All kidding aside, the extra support was great, but it didn't help with slowing down our lives at all. In fact, once we left the hospital, my schedule resumed the usual hectic pace. Now, we were just busy with different things, trading my normal errands for endless trips to the various doctors. It was a little crazy at times trying to maintain some sense of normalcy for Caleb. Thankfully, I had my support system in place to help with a few very basic necessities.

At the time, I was in a women's prayer group at our church and one of my best friends in the group decided to organize meals for us. Mealtimes can be a bit stressful when your kids are small, even more so when coupled with an illness. Their help made dinner time one less thing for me to worry about. My friend set up a rotating schedule, so each person knew the exact day they needed to provide food without her having to make calls every week. She placed a cooler outside our door to give them the freedom to deliver the meal whenever it was convenient for them. The girls who participated even brought everything in non-returnable containers to make it hassle free for us. They literally covered all the bases.

Each of these women had families of their own and yet, in the busyness of their lives, they still found time to reach out to mine. I know it was a sacrifice for each one, yet they did it without fail for four months straight. It was a humbling experience for me and a selfless act for each of them … a labor of love. It was one more way God poured out His blessings on our family and I don't think I have ever felt as treasured as I did during that time. I guess you can say it was another fringe benefit of having cancer!

While trials are hard and no one really wants to walk through them, it is during those times blessings flow and you feel a love that pales in comparison to any other time. It is a pure love and often expressed only when the fear of losing someone arises. I was fortunate to experience that every moment of every day, not only from my family and friends, but from my heavenly Father; for that alone, I wouldn't trade one minute of this journey.

> "Consider it pure joy, my brothers and sisters, whenever you face trials of many kinds, because you know that the testing of your faith produces perseverance. Let perseverance finish its work so that you may be mature and complete, not lacking anything."
>
> James 1:2-4 (NIV)

Threads of Faithfulness

*The Bible calls a woman's hair her crowning glory and the
thought of losing mine was unbearable. I struggled more with
losing my hair than I did with losing my breast. In spite of my
fears surrounding this, once again, God was faithful. Not only
faithful in my search for a wig, but in strengthening my faith
in Him as well.*

NOW WITH THE MASTECTOMY behind me, I focused on more
important issues ... like trying to find a wig for my soon-to-be
bald head! God's faithfulness and provision even in this area
was incredible. Chemotherapy was still a good ten to twelve
weeks away, but with that hanging over my head (no pun
intended) I was a woman on a mission. Always extremely vain
about my hair, I was sure this would be the real test for me.

Initially, I researched ways to try and keep my hair, if possible. Willing to do anything, I even checked into a frozen cap
you could wear while taking treatments that would help lessen
the amount of hair loss. They designed it to freeze the hair

follicles in the hope that it would protect them from the chemotherapy drugs. My oncologist recommended not going that route since he wanted the chemotherapy to reach every single cell possible, even if it meant losing all my hair. As much as I didn't want to, I had to concur.

And so the search for a wig began. I ventured out to any wig salon I could find within a fifty-mile radius. Some were high end salons and a few were less reputable. I tried on everything from blonde, red, to brunette wigs; short styles, long styles and everything in between. But in all the places I searched, there wasn't one wig that made me look like *me*. Nothing looked right and this only magnified the fear growing inside me. By that time I was totally freaking out. What would I do with no hair?

Growing up I had bright, coppery, auburn-colored hair and as a young child and teenager I was less than thrilled about the color God gave me. I always wished for blonde or brown hair, but now that I had the chance to change my hair color, it wasn't nearly as appealing. This is a perfect example of how we women always want what we can't have ... until we get it!

Right before my diagnosis, I was in the process of growing my hair out. It was a frustrating endeavor and I clearly remember wrestling with quite a few bad hair days. However, now, instead of grumbling and complaining about my hair, I was scared to death of losing it. I found myself standing in front of the mirror pleading with God, telling Him, "Okay Lord, this isn't funny! I will never whine about my hair again if you'll just let me keep it. Please ... pretty please ... with sugar on top?" So, I added this to my list of prayers; granted, it wasn't at the top, but it had its rightful place.

After a little digging, we found a company that said they could create an exact replica of your hairstyle using wigs made with real hair! Problem solved. Since they were made to order, it would take a while, but there was time. They were also a bit pricey, but if I had to go through cancer and pregnancy at the same time, I decided to splurge a little so I could at least look good doing it! My husband, being a very loving and kind man (also having survived plenty of my bad hair days), agreed that whatever the cost, it was worth it for me to feel good about myself. What a guy! A thousand dollars later, we ordered the wig and I was sure everything would be great! No more bad hair days; I'd throw the wig on and be out the door. I was actually looking forward to having a *hair recess!*

With that daunting task marked off my list, I wanted to at least try and enjoy my life. The pregnancy progressed nicely and I recuperated from the mastectomy without any complications. In all honesty, it was kind of scary to know I had cancer, and yet I felt incredibly healthy.

Over the next few weeks, God continued to be faithful, placing people in my path to encourage me every step of the way. The more I sought His direction, the more peaceful I became. I'd never experienced this kind of closeness in my walk with the Lord, but then again I never surrendered control to Him this way.

I hungered for more of this newfound peace and looked for ways to draw closer to Him every day. In early spring, I heard that Joyce Meyer planned to come to Hampton, Virginia. Joyce is a Christian Bible teacher, and I enjoyed watching her television program and listening to her tapes. Everyone has a style of teaching that appeals to them and I love Joyce's practical way of getting her points across. I rarely listen to one of her messages where I don't find myself looking out of my window to see if she is watching me. Her transparency makes the Bible totally relatable. Knowing she would be close to where we lived, I thought going to see one of her conferences seemed perfect. Without hesitation, a few of my family members and I decided to take a road trip!

As the weekend drew near, I became more eager to see what God had in store for us. Running on pure adrenalin from the last eight weeks, we desperately needed a special touch. While I sat waiting for the conference to begin, I prayed silently to myself about the cancer and the baby. I will never forget Joyce's opening words that first night. Walking out on stage, she quoted the scripture John 11:40, "Did I not tell you if you would only believe you would see the glory of God?" Adding that she felt like there was someone at the conference who needed to believe what they were praying for.

With ten thousand plus people in attendance, in that moment I felt as if I was the only person standing there and the Lord prompted her to say, "Believe, Melody." I could have left the conference right then completely satisfied that I received what I came for. I jotted the scripture reference down on a piece of paper and tucked it in my Bible. Looking at it several times during the course of the weekend, I pondered the words Jesus spoke to Martha and Mary.

Believe. It sounds simple when you say it, but when you come face to face with a problem, it's nearly impossible to do. I know in my heart that nothing is too big, too small, too insignificant, too anything for God. And yet sometimes I still take my requests before Him, not believing wholeheartedly He will do what I ask. James 1:6-7 tells us, "But when you ask, you must believe and not doubt, because the one who doubts is like a wave of the sea, blown and tossed by the wind. That person should not expect to receive anything from the Lord." So when we pray and then doubt, isn't that praying without faith?

Likewise, the Bible also says if we have faith as small as the grain of a mustard seed and pray, He will answer. He is faithful and He wants us to believe with an innocent, child-like faith … pure and unshakeable. The kind we once so easily relied upon. Faith that says to the world, even though my circumstances might appear otherwise, I believe God is in control.

Up until that point, I wanted to believe everything would be alright, and for the most part I did. But that night, I decided to believe, really believe what I was asking God to do. I know it doesn't make any sense, but I was finding this to be one of the most peaceful times in my life. I went home rejuvenated and ready for the battle waiting for me.

"He will cover you with His feathers, and under His wings you will find refuge; His faithfulness will be your shield and rampart."
Psalm 91:4 (NIV)

18

Threads of Hope

With chemotherapy on the horizon, the baby growing inside of me offered the thread of hope that I needed. The doctors characterized it as a hindrance in my battle to live, but God used the baby to represent the hope I would need to reach down deep and find the strength necessary for the biggest fight of my life.

In the weeks leading up to the treatments, I prayed about whether I should even take the chemotherapy after the healing service we attended. I believed in my heart that God touched my body that night, but how and to what extent I wasn't sure. Did He heal me completely or maybe contain the cancer so it wouldn't spread to my lymph nodes? How could I know for certain? I know God can heal anyone at any time, but I also understand He works through doctors and modern medicine as well. After weighing the pros and cons, we decided to take advantage of all that the medical field had to offer and leave the rest in God's hands.

The time passed quickly and the date for my first treatment arrived. I dreaded this day in some ways and looked forward to it in others. On one hand, I was afraid of being sick, and the thought of losing my hair scared me to death. But on the other hand, I knew taking the treatments would help me win this battle. They were designed to kill any cancer cells that might still be floating through my bloodstream, cells that could potentially kill me if left untreated. I guess you could say it was a love/hate relationship. As I neared my first treatment, I thought about all the stories of fellow cancer survivors being too sick to hold up their heads. Would I experience that, too? And it wasn't just myself I worried about; I was nervous about the effects on the baby, too.

Actually, focusing on the baby instead of the treatments helped to calm my nerves. I was thrilled to finally be pregnant again and concentrating my attention on this tiny miracle provided a wonderful diversion. In the beginning, the pregnancy served as the one thing holding me back from taking the cancer by its ugly horns. Little did I know, this baby would be a light at the end of a dark tunnel. What started out as a hindrance in my battle with cancer soon became my main defense. Hope. I now had someone else to consider in this battle; someone else fighting with me.

May 1, 2001. We headed out that morning filled with a wide array of emotions. First, fear and apprehension regarding the chemotherapy and what that might be like. Then, excitement and anticipation because of the stop we had to make on the way to the cancer center. Before my treatment, we scheduled an appointment to meet with the perinatologist for an ultrasound. Dr. Williams ordered one every few weeks to monitor the baby's progress, and while each one was exciting, we anticipated this one the most.

This ultrasound would reveal whether we were having a boy or a girl. The cancer in no way overshadowed our excitement of finding out the sex of the baby. We were pumped! Everyone placed their bets. Caleb especially wanted to know if he was getting a little brother or a little sister. A brother meant a partner in crime, someone with whom he could seek out trouble, climb trees, and go fishing. On the other hand, with a little sister, things would be altogether different. A girl meant Barbie dolls, makeup, nail polish, lots of screaming, and slumber parties. He went back and forth on which one he wanted more, but either way the idea of being a big brother thrilled him.

Naturally, Rob and I were overjoyed to finally know the gender of the baby, too! As usual, we arrived at the doctor's office with our normal entourage of family members; during this time we seldom traveled alone! Once I was prepped and ready for the procedure, the nurse led everyone into the ultrasound room. Gathering around the bed, all eyes were glued to the screen. I lay on the table for what seemed like an eternity, and since patience isn't my strong suit, I found waiting extremely difficult that day. At last, after checking out all the important stuff, she asked the long-awaited question: "Would you like to know what you're having?"

"Of course we would!" I said.

Just as I rehearsed that moment five years earlier with my son, this moment was no different. Only this time I truly didn't care if it was a boy or a girl. All I wanted was a healthy baby. However, when I heard the words "It's a girl," I thought I would come off the table. My heart rose quickly to the top of my throat. A girl? Did I hear her right? After eleven years, was I really going to have my little girl?

Still, as fast as my heart rose in elation, it sank even faster. I couldn't help but wonder if we were about to relive the same nightmare from eleven years earlier. The doctors warned us that we stood the risk of premature delivery during chemotherapy. Remembering their warning, my mind immediately began to run through all "what-ifs." Surely God wouldn't allow that to happen again, would he? I decided to push those thoughts to the back of my mind and enjoy this long awaited moment. I believed He was in control so far; I needed to continue to trust Him.

When I finally let myself take it in, I could barely contain my excitement. Caleb, on the other hand, didn't share the same enthusiasm! He instantly burst out with an, "Aw, man. Now we are going to have to buy all that Barbie stuff!" This, of course, was followed by everyone in the room bursting into laughter.

As I thought about the baby girl I carried, I realized that God finally answered eleven years of prayer with a yes! I immediately thanked Him for giving Rob and me the courage to trust Him in the beginning. Knowing if I had listened to the doctors and terminated this pregnancy, I wouldn't be having the daughter I dreamed of as a child. I couldn't help but wonder how often God wanted to give me something I prayed for, but I didn't trust Him enough to see it through. I believe God wants to grant us the desires of our hearts, but often that means we have to trust Him...even when everything around us doesn't make any sense.

We left there with a grateful heart, heading to Massey Cancer Center so I could take my first round of chemotherapy. Walking into the treatment center, I felt good physically and emotionally. Rob and I couldn't wait to announce the news regarding the baby to everyone. Dr. Bain and the nurses were ecstatic when we told them we were having a little girl. Throughout the entire ordeal, Rob and I were blessed with the most compassionate doctors and nurses I've ever met. Much like our own family, they embraced us and cared for me in a way I never thought possible. I wasn't sure if it was my pregnancy or my young age. Perhaps both, but I soaked in all the extra attention; it somehow made the process a little more tolerable. Sitting there with my mom and Rob, I was ready to take my first treatment; the sooner we started, the sooner it would be over.

Tara, one of the nurses, opened the door, smiled, and motioned for me to follow her. It was time to start the IV. Given I only had four rounds of chemotherapy to endure I opted not to have a port. Nervously, I sat in the chair waiting for her to begin. I have never really been afraid of needles or shots, but during that time, I grew weary of being stuck. This IV seemed more nerve-racking than usual; perhaps it was just the circumstances surrounding it. No matter how uncomfortable it felt, I understood the necessity of it.

Once she had the IV in place, she started administering the medications into my body. I am not sure what I thought it would feel like when the medicine began trickling down the tube and into my arm, but I felt *absolutely nothing*. It was like receiving any other IV drip of fluids and I found it hard to believe this would have any effect on my cancer. A couple of hours later, I finished the round of chemotherapy and we were free to go. The nurse bade me farewell and said she would see me back in three weeks unless, of course, there were any complications.

As I passed Dr. Bain on my out, he assured me that the next time he saw me I wouldn't have any hair.

"But those who wait on the Lord shall renew their strength; they shall mount up with wings like eagles, they shall run and not be weary, they shall walk and not faint."

Isaiah 40:31 (NKJV)

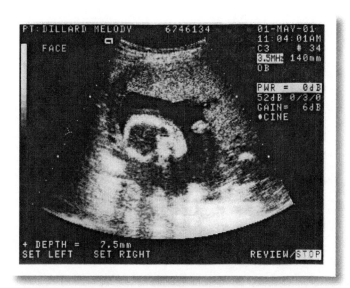

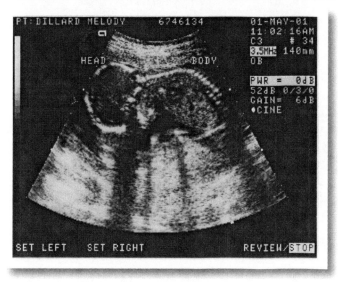

Ultrasound of Avery May 1, 2001

Threads of Humility

A bald head, a bulging belly, and one breast... if that doesn't sew threads of humility into your life, I am not sure what will! Though losing my hair was the most emotionally painful part of my journey, it brought with it a wonderful gift. A new pair of eyes... eyes to recognize others in the same or similar situation as me. They now have one more person praying for them.

DR. BAIN WAS RIGHT. Following my first chemotherapy treatment, my hair slowly began to fall out. I remember standing at the kitchen sink and looking down to see ten or fifteen strands of hair against the white porcelain background. Every day delivered a little more evidence than the day before: on the bathroom counter, my pillow, and sometimes even in the meals I prepared. The shower was probably the worst. As I ran my fingers through my hair to make sure all the shampoo was out, I could feel the strands tangle around my fingers. I prayed and asked God not to let me lose my hair if at all possible, but it appeared losing it was part of His plan.

I knew it wouldn't be long before my hair was so thin others would notice. Before that happened, I wanted one last family picture with my real hair. With little time to spare, we made arrangements to have our picture taken. After that, my common sense finally won out and I decided to have my hair cut into the *cute little pixie* the wig salon recommended. This would allow my hairdresser to cut and style the wig better. Some people look great with short hair; however, I am not one of them. My hair hadn't been that short since I was a little girl. I hated it then, and I hated it now.

And Caleb's reaction when he saw me for the first time only confirmed my feelings. Though we tried to prepare him, at five years old he didn't completely understand the situation. In a way that only a child can do, he took one look at me and said, "Mommy, you look like a little boy!" I knew he didn't mean to hurt me; he was simply stating the obvious. I waited until he left the room, buried my face in a pillow, and sobbed. At that moment, I realized it was time.

Driving Caleb to school the next morning, I decided when I returned home I would ask Rob to shave my head. As I made the loop around the car pool line, I caught another mother looking at me. I was wearing a hat that morning and it was the first time she saw me since I cut my hair. She looked at me and her eyes were full of sympathy and compassion. I could almost hear her heart breaking for me as she watched me drive away. Nonetheless, her expression only reinforced my fear of how people would view me from this point forward.

Driving home, I was hit with the reality of it all.

I walked into the house knowing if I hesitated for even a minute, I might back out. I quickly asked Rob to do the honors. While I sat on the commode in the guest bathroom, Rob made one swipe with his clippers. And then another. I looked down to see pieces of my hair falling all around me. I felt completely vulnerable as my husband looked at me during what I considered the ugliest moment of my life. And for him to perform the act that made me feel that way, I can't even fathom how hard that was for him. It was the most humbling experience of my life, and probably the most intimate moment Rob and I have shared in our marriage. Seeing my hair hit the floor that morning was harder than I ever imagined it would be.

Rob, however, never ceased to amaze me. There really are no words sufficient to describe this man's attitude and heart towards me during that time. Men are visual creatures. God designed them to be stimulated by outward appearances. Rob went from having a wife he found physically attractive, to having a wife with one breast, a bulging belly (among other bulging things), and a bald head. Someone fit for a science fiction film without any help from the makeup and wardrobe departments!

Still, Rob looked at me the same way he did the day we were married. How is that possible? I wondered. Not once did Rob ever make me feel unattractive; in fact, he chased me around the house just as much as he did before the cancer. The unconditional love he showed me during that time was the closest example of Christ's love for me that I have ever experienced from another human. In a way I have yet to understand, Rob made me feel like the most beautiful woman in the world.

How I viewed myself? That was a different story altogether. Let's just say, no woman should ever have to see herself without hair. For the first time since I was diagnosed, I looked and felt like a cancer patient. Every time I saw my reflection in the mirror, I was reminded of the cancer. The mastectomy had left behind a sunken spot with the skin stretched tightly over my rib cage. Now, I had a bald head to go along with my emaciated chest. Neither ever got any easier to look at, but at least covering my chest was a simple fix compared to hiding my bald head. Anywhere I went required a decision. Do I wear the wig? A hat, or perhaps a scarf? I thought this *hair recess* would be a breeze, but let me tell you, I couldn't have been more wrong! Without a doubt, there are women who embrace the whole scarf thing, but not me.

I am sure that there weren't nearly as many people looking at me as I thought, but I felt like I was in a giant fish bowl with the whole world staring at me. After all, how many pregnant women do you see wearing a scarf and hat? And regrettably, the wig that was supposed to be the answer to all of my hair dilemmas created more stress than relief. I wanted so badly to look like myself again; I thought I was making a good choice in getting one made with real hair. But since human hair wigs are equally as sensitive to humidity as your own hair, I found myself washing and styling it almost every day. Talk about stress; it was unbelievable!

Occasionally, I was able to find a little humor in it, as when Caleb would rub my head and kiss it, telling me he liked it that way. Or during his bath time, I would lean over the tub so he could pour water on my head just to watch it bead up and roll off. Of course, now I look back and cherish those moments, but at the time I cringed. As shallow as it might sound, I cried more over losing my hair than my breast. I know it's crazy... hair grows back, breasts don't. I even asked myself numerous times, "When you are fighting for your life, who really cares about hair?" Nevertheless, I continued to answer, "Me." Looking back, I know I placed more significance on it than it rightfully deserved, but at the time it seemed monumental.

Up until this period in my life, I gave little thought about what it would be like to not have any hair. Most of the time I was so focused on myself that I never noticed the woman at the grocery store wearing a scarf. Such a small detail about someone else never caught my attention... until I *became* that woman wearing the scarf.

There are few times now that I don't notice that woman. Wondering what she is going through, I silently lift her up in prayer.

> "Therefore He says: 'God resists the proud but gives grace to the humble.'"
>
> James 4:6 (NKJV)

Last family picture taken before I lost my hair May 2001

Rob and Melody
in the summer
and fall of 2001
with Melody
sporting her wig

Threads of Transition

This time was characterized by one transition after another. My treatments were almost over and while that was a good thing, it was an adjustment. The loss of my hair and the anticipation of our new arrival remained at the forefront of my mind. I barely had time to process all the changes that were taking place.

WITH THREE OF THE FOUR treatments under my belt, my body tolerated the drugs remarkably well. Dr. Bain took extra precautions to ensure I didn't experience many of the normal side effects that accompany chemotherapy. He prescribed a steroid and an anti-nausea medicine, and together, these two medicines functioned to help me maintain a stable and healthy diet. Dr. Bain understood the importance of my being able to eat, not only for myself but for the baby.

It worked perfectly! In fact, I never missed a single meal, and aside from some really bad constipation and losing my hair, I wouldn't have even known I was taking chemotherapy.

Well, that is, if you don't consider the insane number of doctor's appointments. My first chemotherapy treatment was on May 1st and that month alone, I had twelve appointments. Aside from feeling a little tired due to my schedule, I honestly didn't experience the usual fatigue that accompanies chemotherapy. Surely, God put a hedge of protection around me!

Finally, we neared the home stretch with my last treatment scheduled for Thursday, July 5th. At eighteen weeks pregnant when I started the first treatment, by the time I reached my last round, I was twenty-seven weeks into the pregnancy. Up until that point, everything was smooth sailing. But from the moment that week began to unfold, it proved to be an emotional one. It started first with blood work to check and make sure all my levels were good enough to take my final treatment and an X-ray to look at my lungs. Aside from the X-ray producing quite a bit of anxiety, everything checked out okay. I prepared for my last treatment and took a deep breath, certain the worst was over.

However, we soon discovered we weren't in the clear quite yet. Our summers here in Virginia are hot and humid, so enduring pregnancy during the summer can be pretty miserable. But being pregnant and wearing a wig in the summer is almost unbearable. In spite of all that we had going on, Rob and I decided Caleb needed swimming lessons! I know it sounds bizarre and even a bit untimely; nonetheless, I accepted the responsibility of taking him. I vividly remember the morning of his first session just like it was yesterday. Watching his instructor work with him, I sat near the edge of the pool with the sun bearing down on me, ready to spontaneously combust. I could feel the temperature in my body rising, but with the wig in place there was no way for it to escape.

After they finished, we headed straight to the truck and I cranked the AC on full blast trying to cool off. I couldn't wait to remove the wig, but since I didn't have a hat or scarf with me I left it in place. Once I walked through the door of my house, I immediately peeled it off and reached for my bandana. I didn't like the look of the bandana, but it was always a welcome relief after wearing the wig for even a short time. It had been a long morning and I was a bit fatigued, but nothing that sent up a red flag. As the afternoon went on I started feeling much better and gave little thought to the episode that morning.

However, when I arrived at my doctor's appointment the next day, the nurse practitioner examined me only to discover I was having some contractions. Perhaps because of the heat, or maybe just the fact that I don't ever drink enough water, I was dehydrated. Before I knew what was happening, I found myself ushered down to labor and delivery and hooked up to half a dozen monitors and an IV. I guess sitting in ninety-degree weather while pregnant and wearing a wig wasn't such a great combination.

Given my past history and the fact I was only twenty-seven weeks along, I should have been freaking out, but for whatever reason I remained relatively calm. Again, I say it was a *God* thing. Rob arrived shortly after they got me settled and, as always, he was cool and collected. Dr. Williams was off this particular day, so the on-call physician came in periodically to check on things. With a few phone calls, we knew hundreds of prayers were going up on our behalf. Once I was well hydrated, the contractions tapered off and they sent us home. Expelling yet another huge sigh of relief, I was grateful it was nothing more serious. What a week, I thought ... first, the X-ray of my lungs and now this. And I still had one more treatment to go.

My chemo usually fell on Thursdays, and as you can imagine, by the time this Thursday rolled around, my emotions were spent. I didn't even realize exactly how much until that morning as I got ready to leave for the hospital. It wasn't any different than the other days I took treatments, except for the fact I couldn't stop crying. That week held such a wide range of emotions, I was having a hard time dealing with it all. This was my last of four treatments. It should have been a time of relief and celebration, yet it completely overwhelmed me. Breaking down like this was totally out of character for me, and I struggled to pinpoint exactly what was wrong. All attempts to pull myself together before we got to the cancer center proved futile.

From the moment I walked through the doors until we left, I cried. While the nurse inserted the IV, while the drugs were administered into my body, and as she removed the needle from my arm for the last time I was a blubbering mess! And when Tara presented me with a pink, plush breast cancer teddy bear, I couldn't even utter one word. The water-works turned up to a whole new level! I guess now, as I look back, it was probably a multitude of things rather than just the events of that particular week. We'd been through so much over the last five months; the strain wore on me as things were coming to an end.

With all the treatments finally behind us, Rob and I decided to squeeze in a quick trip to the beach before the baby arrived. Even though I recognized we needed the time to get away and catch our breath, I wasn't exactly all that excited about flaunting my well rounded body up and down the beach, especially given the fact that I knew most of the other girls would barely have anything on. But, more than my baby bump, I guess the full head dress bothered me the most. I knew wearing the wig wasn't practical, but at least no one would have noticed me with hair. Nonetheless, I pushed aside my insecurities and we headed to the beach.

However, from the second my feet hit that hot white sand, I wondered why we didn't sneak away to the mountains instead. Talk about sticking out like a sore thumb! There I was, looking like someone straight out of Hollywood in full disguise. I wore a black maternity swimsuit complete with a sheer overlay... and of course, black sunglasses. I felt safer not making eye contact with anyone. My hat was a wide brimmed straw hat with a black sheer sash that fell down and touched the top of my shoulders. Do you have a visual yet? It looked like Jackie O had hit the beach! I'm not kidding. Everyone was looking at me, as if they were trying to figure out who I was...or at least

I thought they were. As it turned out, Rob and I did have fun and enjoyed relaxing for a few days.

The worst was over and we could now focus on getting ready for our new addition.

> "Come to me, all you who labor and are heavy laden, I will give you rest."
>
> Matthew 11:28 (NKJV)

Picture of me incognito at Lake Gaston summer 2001

21

Threads of Believing

Believe. Sounds simple enough, yet it's nearly impossible to do when your immediate circumstances show otherwise... unless you are trusting God. In the beginning we confronted an impossible situation, but we prayed, we believed, and we saw His glory in the birth of a long-awaited miracle.

WITH OCTOBER 3ʳᵈ AS MY ACTUAL due date, I never thought I would go full term. Leighton came sixteen weeks early and Caleb one week early; I couldn't imagine this pregnancy would be any different. I waited a long time to be pregnant both times, so I definitely wanted to savor every moment expectant moms find pleasure in. I don't think there is any time in a woman's life when she feels more special than while carrying a baby. In spite of this cancer, I truly enjoyed everything about this pregnancy.

Still, as September drew closer, my anticipation mounted and I could hardly wait to hold my little girl. I worked on getting the nursery ready, and making sure it was fit for a princess! But despite my busyness, those last few weeks somehow felt longer than the whole nine months. Each visit to the doctor left me more anxious than the previous one. Dr. Williams and his nurses did a wonderful job of making me feel special during the whole pregnancy. He always found a way to make me laugh in spite of the situation, even over my hair! I looked forward to each visit and, as strange as it may sound, I knew I would feel sad when it was all over.

Nearing the third week of September, something finally started to happen. My appointments earlier in the month indicated I was beginning to dilate. First one centimeter, then two. Then, on September 19th, it happened! This particular day was busy, filled with everything from running errands, doing laundry, picking Caleb up from school, and even a little yard work. And that evening was just like any other school night at our house... hectic. It was always a little challenging getting ready for the next day with dinner, bath, and homework. When I finally took a minute to stop, I noticed a light pink discharge. Dismissing it until I got Caleb settled in bed, I decided to call my OB/GYN and ask a few questions. Of course, since it was after regular business hours I was directed to their answering service. The receptionist ran through the normal questions and told me Dr. Williams would call soon.

I was surprised to learn that he was actually the one on-call that night. After I explained my symptoms, since he was already at the hospital he offered to induce me if Rob and I wanted to come in. Naturally, with my lack of patience, I was ready to grab my bag and head out the door. However, Rob, the more levelheaded of us, said, "Are you crazy, Melody? We can't go tonight, Caleb is asleep and he has school tomorrow. Call Dr. Williams back and ask him if we can come first thing in the morning." Although I was disappointed, I knew he was right. With a few phone calls, we let everyone know the latest development and prepared to have our baby. I hardly slept that night in anticipation of the following day and all that it would hold.

Bright and early the next morning, we headed for St. Mary's hospital. Having made this trip numerous times throughout my battle with cancer, I found this ride completely different from all the others. I was excited to finally see my baby, but also elated Dr. Williams would be the one delivering her. With both of my previous pregnancies, my regular doctors weren't available when I went into labor. Dr. Williams had been right there beside Rob and me every step of the way. He played such an important role in this journey, and I would have been heartbroken if he wasn't the one to deliver my baby. My mom always says that a woman falls in love with the doctor who delivers her baby. Not in a literal sense, of course, but in an idyllic way. I definitely felt a special bond with Dr. Williams, and I considered it a blessing that he would be the one sharing in this momentous occasion with us!

His crazy personality immediately put Rob at ease. Once we were settled, they eagerly chatted about my status, and Dr. Williams told Rob about the special concoction he uses to help with the delivery process. And, of course, he took great care in making sure I was comfortable ... kind of. He and I enjoyed a different doctor/patient relationship in the way we sarcastically joked back and forth with one another. In fact, when he broke my water, it hurt more than I expected and as I dug my toes into his side, he let out a shout! Obviously, I was all over that, letting him know I was the one in labor, not him. We all shared a good laugh, and Rob even remarked, "I can't believe we are having a baby right now." The atmosphere was so relaxing I remember telling them both what a wonderful time I was having! I guess the Lord figured that after all I'd been through in the last nine months I should enjoy a peaceful delivery.

On September 20, 2001, at 11:02 a.m., Gracelyn Avery blessed us with her presence. After facing months of uncertainty from the medical field, she was finally here, safe and sound. Not to mention, she was perfect. More beautiful than I ever imagined, I knew from the moment they laid her in my arms she was a princess. She weighed 6 lbs. 9 oz. and was 20 inches long. Truly a miracle, there was simply no way you could look at Avery and not see the glory of God. He made a way where there was no way. As I held her in my arms, His goodness and provision overwhelmed me. I knew I was blessed far beyond what I deserved.

And Caleb was at last a big brother, a role he couldn't wait to embrace. Without a doubt, he asked God for a little brother or sister long before I learned I was pregnant. At only five years old, he was such a faithful prayer warrior, praying for not only me and the cancer, but also for the health of his unborn baby sister. I am not sure he fully understood God's actions during this period, but his childlike faith never wavered. It was good for him to see God's provision and faithfulness.

Indeed in the beginning, we wondered, What are you doing God? A baby and cancer? But with God, nothing is impossible. Holding Avery was a confirmation that God had completed what He started. We claimed the scripture John 11:40: "Did I not tell you if you would only believe you would see the glory of God?" We prayed. We believed. God was faithful. After losing one child and trying tirelessly to have another, I deem all babies a miracle from heaven. However, after battling cancer while carrying one, I truly believe her life gives new meaning to the word "miracle."

God heard and answered all the prayers we lifted up throughout the year.

> "Did I not tell you if you believe, you will see the glory of God?"
>
> John 11:40 (NIV)

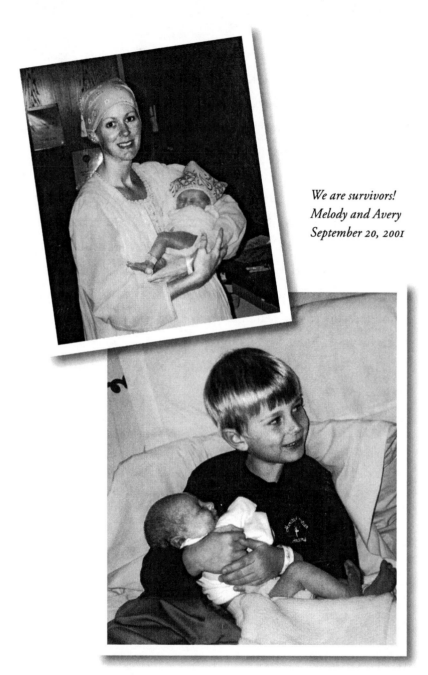

We are survivors!
Melody and Avery
September 20, 2001

Proud big brother! Caleb and Avery September 20, 2001

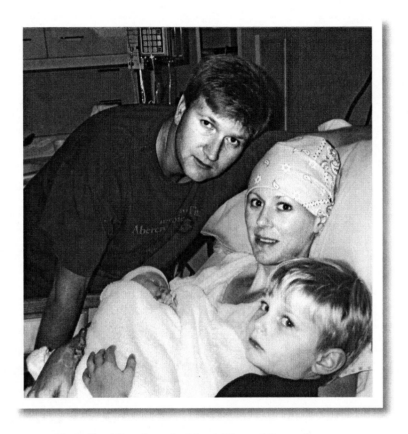

The Dillard Family at St. Mary's Hospital September 2001

Threads of Love

With Avery here, our hearts overflowed with love. I'd dreamt of having a little girl all my life. And after losing Leighton eleven years earlier, my dream seemed to die with her. Indeed, God granted my heart's desire to have a child when He blessed me with a son. Now, He was fulfilling my childhood wish to have a little girl… it was truly like having the whipped cream and cherry on top!

As we prepared to take Avery home from the hospital, my heart was full with excitement and gratitude. I waited over eleven years to finally have a little girl, and I had to pinch myself to be sure she wasn't a figment of my imagination. Dressed in one of my own baby dresses, she looked like an angel. Her face was so tiny you could barely see it hidden inside the lacey bonnet.

In addition, my mind was reeling with ideas about the birth announcement! Every mother loves to announce the arrival of their new bundle of joy. While I couldn't wait to share the news with everyone, more importantly, I wanted to give God the glory. I'd decided months earlier to use the scripture we claimed all year, John 11:40. It only made sense; when I divulged my idea to Rob and my mom, they agreed it was perfect. As we drove home, I began creating the preliminary draft in my head.

Once home, I settled Avery in her bassinette and decided to get caught up on a few things. Due to all the excitement at the hospital, I had fallen behind on my devotions. Knowing how precious alone time can be, I stretched across Caleb's bed and nuzzled up to one of his pillows. Opening my *Streams in the Desert* devotional, I turned to page 357. I'd stopped reading at September 19th, the day before Avery's arrival. When I opened the book, my eyes caught the words printed at the bottom of the page. I couldn't believe what it said. In fact, I did a double take to make sure I wasn't seeing things. The scripture reading for September 20th was John 11:40. My scripture. My first thoughts were, You have got to be kidding me, God. How is this possible?

I don't think I have ever experienced God's presence like I did at that moment. I felt as though He was standing right there beside me saying, "See, Melody? I told you if you would only trust Me, I would take care of everything." Running down the stairs to show my mom, I stood beside her in utter amazement, not knowing what to say or think. When I finally collected my composure, I called my pastor. He shared the same sentiment... it was no coincidence. With over 31,000 verses in the Bible and countless devotional books on bookshelves everywhere, who could do that but God?

I felt humbled, humbled that the Creator of the universe cared enough about me to orchestrate something of this magnitude. Taking the time to impress upon this author's heart to choose this particular verse as the scripture reading for September 20th, then prompting my step-sister, Robin, to give me that very devotional. Likewise, God used several people to speak that verse to me in such profound ways throughout the year, it caused me to take note and claim it. He then planned my delivery perfectly so that Avery would be born on that very day, and two weeks early at that. Some would call all of this a coincidence when, really, I knew it was another precious miracle in my life.

My feeling is God coordinated all this so I would know beyond a shadow of a doubt that He was in control and loved me more than I could possibly imagine. Just one more blessing in the midst of what started out as a complete nightmare. As if all He had done over the last nine months wasn't enough! I wondered many times that year how God had time for anyone else since He was so busy taking care of me. I honestly felt like I was the apple of His eye.

Realizing all this made me even more anxious to get the birth announcements out to proclaim God's goodness to everyone. And while I prioritized that, making sure I got the princess on a feeding schedule took precedence as well. Understanding how important it was for me to breastfeed Avery, Dr. Bain agreed to postpone starting the oral cancer medication for six months. I nursed Caleb, and though I worried about having enough milk with only one breast, I wanted to try and nurse Avery too. Caleb and I formed such a special bond as a result of this closeness, I couldn't imagine not sharing that experience with her.

Without a doubt, watching Avery nurse was one of the most precious sights I have ever seen. I know it sounds strange to describe it like this, but her spirit and countenance were so humble, as though she appeared grateful. As I held her in my arms, she would look up at me and promptly reach for my hand, wrapping her tiny little fingers around one of mine. It was without measure, and I cherished her expressions of love for me.

After my milk came in, I produced enough for twins, even with only one breast. In fact, I pumped most days in between her regular feedings. By the time I started the oral medication, I had at least a month's reserve in the freezer. Truthfully, it was unbelievable!

Once my hair began to grow back, I didn't always wear the wig at home. When I fed her without it, she would stare at me with a puzzled look on her face, as if to say, "Who is this strange woman feeding me?" However, she must have approved because she continued nursing! I would give anything to know her thoughts during those moments.

I loved every part that went along with taking care of Avery. Having waited so long to finally have a little girl, sometimes I could hardly believe she was really mine. Whenever I went to change her diaper, I found myself looking at her little bottom and thinking, She really is a girl!

Our family was at last complete.

"And now these three remain: faith, hope and love. But the greatest of these is love."

1 Corinthians 13:13 (NIV)

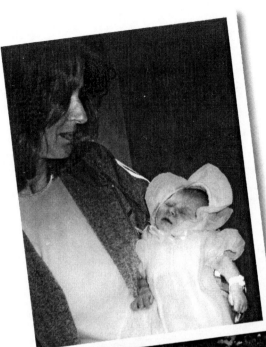

*Avery getting ready
to leave the hospital
September 22, 2001*

*Proud big brother!
Caleb and Avery
taking a stroll
September 2001*

Avery wrapping her fingers around mine March 2002

Threads of Restoration

Before I knew it, the time to have my reconstructive surgery arrived. Though the process was long and painful, I needed and wanted to look like a whole woman again. If not for myself, I desired it for my husband who had stood by my side throughout this ordeal.

WITH A NEW BABY and a five-year-old to keep me busy, I lost track of the days. Thanksgiving was quickly approaching, and considering how much we had to be thankful for, I planned Avery's dedication for the weekend after. My hair was growing back nicely, and that Sunday morning was my first time showing off my new military style hairdo. Though I didn't like the way it looked, the freedom of not wearing anything offered the first outward sign of life after cancer.

As we prepared to head into the holiday season, I was certain the worst was behind us. Then one morning while taking a shower, I encountered some tenderness around my ribcage. Located on the same side as the cancer, it made me a little nervous. I called Dr. Bain's office and left a message with his nurse. Dr. Bain called back later that afternoon and suggested I have a full body scan to check and see if the cancer had spread to any of my bones. I knew all along the chance of it entering my bloodstream existed, but I didn't think I would be facing this possibility just yet.

Immediately, my thoughts ran rampant with all the different scenarios. While I experienced a tremendous amount of peace most of the time, there were a few moments when my human-ness overruled. It was during those times that my mind shifted into overdrive planning my own funeral service … choosing the songs and writing the eulogy … you know the whole bit. I am sure you have been there and done that at one point in your life, even if you have never been diagnosed with cancer. It is crazy how the mind works!

Nonetheless, we headed back to the hospital and I realized this cancer would always be there, waiting to rear its ugly head. Now any time something surfaced, no matter how small, it would require further evaluation. Aches and pains once easily dismissed would, instead, require a colossal number of tests. The concern of reoccurrence would always hover in the back-ground, no matter how much I tried to put everything behind me. It was my new normal. I tried to process these truths as we waited for them to take me back to begin the procedure.

The test required them to inject me with a radioactive dye in order to acquire the results they needed. Normally, this wouldn't have been a big deal, except I was still nursing. Since having the test wasn't optional, I decided to pump and throw the milk away for three days until my body could rid itself of the dye. It broke my heart to pour all that milk out, especially only having one breast; it was like throwing away liquid gold! Thankfully, I had my reserve in the freezer, and in the end everything worked out fine.

The results from the scan came back clean and Avery was such a little trooper. She went from nursing to taking a bottle and then back to nursing, never missing a beat. But with her laid back disposition, that didn't really come as a surprise to any of us. Some people believe that how peaceful the mom is during her pregnancy influences the baby's temperament. That may be an old wives' tale, but from the moment Avery was born, she was as peaceful a baby as I was a pregnant mom. She loved when I held her or was fine when I put her down. She was even content to lay for long stretches under her activity bar while swatting at her dangling toys.

Those first six months flew by, and Avery seemed to grow right before my very eyes. The date for me to stop nursing and begin taking my oral medication came too soon. I nursed Caleb until he was a year old, and even though I knew from the start that wasn't a possibility with Avery, it still didn't make it any easier. As the end neared, I was grateful for what time we had, but sad that I would never know that feeling again.

However, the end of this phase marked the beginning of a new one. The reconstructive process! Up until that point, I had been wearing a breast enhancer a friend gave me that just slipped down inside my bra. Since I knew surgery was in the near future, I didn't see any need to order a prosthetic insert. And other than the fact that it would occasionally fall out if I bent over too far, it wasn't all that bad.

Dr. Bain recommended I go through genetic testing first, to see if I carried the gene for breast cancer. He thought that would be helpful in deciding whether I should have my other breast removed during the reconstructive process. I really didn't need a genetic test to help me decide; if the insurance company would pay for it, I wanted it gone. It was a no-brainer for me.

Besides, I wanted them to look the same. Who wants one perky breast and one saggy, mushy one that had breastfed two babies? Not me. Nonetheless, I knew finding out whether I carried the gene or not would help determine if I was at risk for any other type of cancer. The results of this type of testing are usually accurate within a twelve percent margin of error, and it was a huge relief when my report came back indicating I was not a carrier.

In spite of the outcome, our insurance company generously approved a prophylactic mastectomy. And so my search for a reconstructive surgeon commenced. One might think choosing the physician in charge of reconstructing your breasts is stressful, but I didn't find it nearly as difficult as settling on the wig! Some of my nurses and doctors gave us several names of highly recommended plastic surgeons, but one name kept coming up over and over: Dr. Mara LaRoche. When I learned she was a woman, I was a little reluctant after my experience with Leighton. But, given the fact that everyone we talked to said she was the best in her field, I put my reservations aside and made the appointment. Mentally and physically, I was ready to get things moving. After all, by this time fourteen months had passed since my mastectomy.

It was early June, 2002, before I could get an appointment with Dr. LaRoche. While eager to go, I still had many questions about the process, as well as concerns about seeing a female doctor again. However, since I am not much of a researcher, I did very little digging on my upcoming surgeries or the types of implants that were available. Instead, I saved all my questions for the consultation.

Once the day arrived, Rob and I checked in at the front desk and her nurse led us back to one of the examination rooms. We waited anxiously, listening for the shuffle of papers being removed from the plastic holder on the door. Finally, I could hear her flipping through my chart. Opening the door she looked at me, her face unable to mask her thoughts. "Oh my God, you're so young!" she exclaimed. Her big brown eyes were filled with compassion and there was gentleness in her voice. My anxieties suddenly diminished, and from that moment on, I knew we made the right decision.

Dr. LaRoche was petite in her frame and appeared much younger than I envisioned, too. Her hair was pulled into a loose, messy bun that morning and stray pieces fell on either side of her cheeks. She wore very little make-up; there was nothing fake or pretentious about her. Down to earth in the way she spoke, she talked openly about her kids and family, asking me about mine as well. We shared an immediate connection and I sensed she genuinely cared about me and my circumstances.

After examining me, she described what the reconstructive process would entail. It wasn't nearly as simple as just going in and inserting the implants like I hoped. There were several different phases and she carefully expounded upon each one of them. My first reconstructive surgery involved Dr. Caldwell removing my remaining breast and Dr. LaRoche putting the expanders in place. The expanders were used to re-stretch my skin, enabling it to accept the implant. I never quite understood the whole purpose behind them, since they looked almost exactly like the actual implant. Why not put them in right away? It didn't make a lot of sense to me, but then again, a lot of things during the last eighteen months were a little hard to comprehend.

Seeing how I breezed through my last two surgeries, I expected to sail through these as well. Still, given the fact that I elected to do these next few surgeries, the potential complications troubled me. With the mastectomy, I didn't have time to worry about all the possible issues. Everything happened so quickly and there really was no choice if I wanted to survive. I tried not to dwell on all the possibilities since I knew going through this process was the only way I could look like a whole woman again. Once I learned Dr. LaRoche and Dr. Caldwell had worked together previously, it helped to put my mind at ease as well. With everything coming together so smoothly, I was beginning to get more excited about the surgeries.

Even though Rob never gave the impression my appearance bothered him, I'd grown weary of seeing my disfigured body in the mirror. We were both only thirty-four at the time I was diagnosed and I couldn't imagine growing old like this. Besides, I didn't want Rob to go the next fifty-plus years with his wife having only one breast. He deserved better than that. I wanted to look like the woman he married, so we scheduled the initial surgery for the first part of August.

When I came to after that first surgery and the pain medication began to wear off, my chest ached as though I had been beaten unmercifully with a baseball bat. The intensity of the pain was so much greater than with my previous surgeries, I was taken aback. Dr. LaRoche did quite a bit of cutting into my chest wall to create pockets to slip the expanders down in, which caused most of my agony. During those first eight or ten days, it basically hurt to breathe. I couldn't even manage to get myself out of bed without my mom or Rob helping me to my feet. Though I knew it would all be worth it in the end, this was definitely more difficult than the mastectomy. With each day that passed, the tenderness lessened. I was thankful to have all the extra help, and before too long I was up and moving. As usual, my mom and Rob were awesome! And when I was too sore to pick up Avery, Caleb would happily tote her around as long as his little arms would allow.

We scheduled the next surgery for February, 2003. I have to admit, with the severity of the pain, I was grateful for the reprieve. Anxious to start working again, I took on an occasional decorating job. Soon, I was faux finishing furniture again. And taking care of Caleb and Avery kept me quite busy, too. Just as Caleb assumed the role of Bible Man, Avery embraced the role of a princess! It's not easy being the mother of a *princess* you know. There are costume changes several times a day and tea parties to attend! On certain days Avery was Cinderella, and on others Sleeping Beauty. In fact, having blond hair and blue eyes, many times she would look at pictures of Sleeping Beauty and ask me, "Is dat me, Mommy? Dat me?" Of course, I would respond, "Yes, Honey. That's you!" Occasionally, you could even catch her wearing her cowgirl boots with a princess dress while swinging on our tire swing, which naturally earned her the title of *The Farm Princess*. When I asked God for a girl, He truly outdid Himself.

And as for Avery's temperament, it was the complete opposite of her brother's! Not nearly as determined to have things her way, she was laid back and easy going. Except, of course, when she stood in between my legs crying, "Hold you Mommy, hold you." Avery was an absolute joy to be around and she soon became my little sidekick.

The next two surgeries were, thankfully, uneventful. On February 27th, Dr. LaRoche put in the actual set of implants. This surgery wasn't nearly as painful as the last, and the recovery was quite a bit easier, too. A few months later, in June, she performed the nipple reconstruction. I found it incredible that they could create a nipple out of nothing. But they can! When she asked me if I wanted a permanently *hard* or *soft* nipple, I couldn't help but laugh. Of all the choices I made during my life, I never imagined myself making that one. Overall, everything turned out well, as far as the reconstructive process went. Some of my cousins even joke that I will be ninety years old and still have a pair of fifteen-year-old breasts! I guess one could classify that as looking at the glass half-full instead of half-empty! Whatever they look like now or when I am ninety, I am just glad to have them, as well as my health.

With a few surgeries and quite a bit of soreness, I began to look more like a whole woman again.

> "Lord, by such things people live; and my spirit finds life in them too. You restored me to health and let me live."
>
> Isaiah 38:16 (NIV)

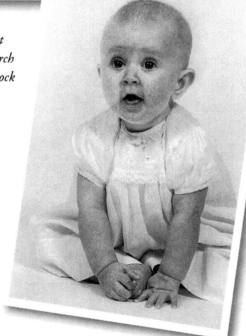

Avery's baby dedication at
Southside Nazarene Church
with Pastor Jerome Hancock
on November 25, 2001

Avery at six months
old March 2002

Feeling like Cinderella today!

Melody and Avery at The Fairytale Ball

One of Avery's many tea parties with Brown Bear on our back porch

Threads of Peace

With the reconstructive process finished, God would soon carry out a work of greater magnitude... a spiritual restoration. The peace I experienced during my battle with cancer truly surpassed all understanding. However, with that time coming to a close, I loosened my grip on God's hand and I saw those threads quickly begin to unravel. Though not right away, I finally realized what I needed to do to mend the broken threads.

AS THIS SEASON OF OUR LIFE came to a close, it was a time filled with more blessings than our hearts could measure. Two years earlier, I would have never imagined myself looking back on this as a time I would cherish, but I did.

Still, it felt amazing to reclaim the normalcy we enjoyed before my cancer; I didn't realize just how much I missed our ordinary life. Rob focused on work, my business flourished, the kids grew, and God blessed us all with good health. Sadly, along with our lives returning to their original state, so did our relationship with the Lord.

Little by little we gradually became more relaxed in our walk. *Gradual* and *little* being the key words. More often than not, that is exactly how Satan works. If he moves too quickly, it may send up a red flag, bringing about awareness and throwing a kink in his plan. I guess it's kind of like the story about the frog that the cook puts into the pot of water. If the water was at a boiling temperature when you put him in, he would be inclined to jump right back out. But by increasing the temperature slowly, the frog never even realizes what's happening.

Rob and I were similar to the frog. It wasn't that we made a conscious choice to loosen our grip on God's hand, but we didn't make an intentional decision to keep holding it either. We allowed the busyness of life to creep back in, dictating how and where we spent our time. Making small compromises in seemingly unimportant areas, before I knew it, we reached a place of total complacency with God.

While we still went to church (on Sunday mornings), prayed (about some things), dropped a check in the offering plate (most of the time for an amount I felt comfortable with) and lived a basically moral life, Rob and I didn't keep Him first. You know, kind of "playing church." Like a lot of Christians today, we were neither hot nor cold, but rather lukewarm.

It took time to reach that place and unfortunately, even longer to recognize we were there. Looking back now, it's difficult for me to imagine how we allowed that to happen after all God did for me with my cancer. But the Old Testament of the Bible speaks of many occasions when kings and leaders obeyed

God's commands for a period of time and then turned their worship to false idols.

One morning while reading some of these stories, I became quite frustrated. Looking at account after account, I wondered why they continued to waver in their faith. What don't they get? I thought. When they obey Him, He devours their enemies and they triumph. When they turn away and worship false idols, they endure His wrath. It's really a no-brainer.

After contemplating further, I realized I was just like them. Trusting and seeking God during the storms of life, once I reach the shores of safety, I let Him know that I am ready to take the wheel again. With my actions, I proclaim loud and clear He won't be needed that day, instead, allowing my own plans and desires to come first.

While we don't carve wooden images or cast idols out of gold today, we do have our own brand of idols: our house, our work, our toys... even relationships. It is not an easy thing to talk about or admit, and it certainly doesn't make us feel very good, but I know I have mine. These obsessions in our life are what take our focus off of Him.

Holding them in such high regard, even after all God did for me through my battle with cancer, I allowed these idols to take priority over Him. In the same way God gave the leaders in the Old Testament the freedom to turn from Him, He permits us to do the same. Our freedom to choose is a gift; God will never force Himself on anyone. Although that might sound great, in reality, it is the reason so many of us wander around in our own wilderness for years, trying to accomplish what God could easily do in a short amount of time.

Once I realized my mistake, I began making changes. There was only one problem. Instead of surrendering myself totally to God, I was trying *on my own* to be a good Christian. I wasn't allowing *Him* to change me into the person He wanted me to be. After all, that's really what it's about ... surrender. He desires for each of us to come to a place of total surrender by our own submission. By the time I finish this book, I will have already lived half of my life. And I am sorry to say that it has taken me that long to completely surrender my life to the Lord.

When I was diagnosed with cancer, I surrendered *that situation* to God. I sought Him for direction in every decision and He honored that. But God longs for more than a moment or a season in our life, He actually asks that we give Him *our whole life*. That means our heart, our friendships, our marriage, our children, and yes, our finances. Complete surrender, total abandonment of our will. Our will is strong and not easily broken!

As 2011 came to a close, mine crumbled. Already making small changes in my life, I could see God working. Yet, I still wasn't enjoying the same peace I did when I had cancer. Reaching the end of my rope, so to speak, I confessed to God, "I can't do this anymore." If what I was experiencing was all life had to offer, I truly didn't care to be a part of it.

Now, I am not implying that I considered taking my own life; I simply reached a place where nothing really mattered, a place void of joy and peace. I found myself going through the motions each day because my family depended on me, not because I derived any pleasure from it. And the saddest part of all? I had no reason to be unhappy. Blessed with my health, a wonderful husband, a teenage son I actually love being around, the daughter I always dreamed of, a flourishing business, and a beautiful home, what more could someone want? Sound familiar?

At this point, my hunger for peace was so great that I truthfully felt if my cancer ever came back that I would be okay. "Okay" because the year I was sick was the most peaceful time of my life. I longed for that same feeling over and over during the last ten years, even verbalizing my sentiments to a handful of my closest friends. Then standing at the foot of my bed folding clothes one afternoon, I sensed the Holy Spirit say to me, "Melody, you don't have to have cancer to enjoy that same peace; you just have to seek Me like you did then." I knew all along it wasn't Him that had moved; rather, it was me.

And so this brings us to January, 2012. A year I vowed to live differently than 2011 and every other! Determined not to continue on the *treadmill of life*, I set out on a new journey in search of peace; I probably shouldn't use the word *search*, since that implies one doesn't know where something is. I knew where I lost it and exactly where to find it. In order for me to find the kind of contentment I longed for, though, it would require time: time to be quiet and listen; time to read my Bible and fellowship with the Lord like I once did; time that I had chosen to devote to other things and people.

I experienced peace *with* God through my salvation as a little girl, but up until this point, I'd not really enjoyed the peace *of* God in my life. There is a difference. Discovering this distinction may be one of the most important lessons I've learned on this journey. You can't enjoy the peace of God in your life unless you have surrendered your whole self to Him. However, that doesn't always happen at the time you receive Christ into your heart; instead, it is a work He does in and through you over time, transforming you into a new creation until the person you once were slowly dies out.

As I began to seek God and His direction, I savored my newfound peace. In fact, on the mornings I fail to spend time with Him, I sense a significant change in my attitude and how my day goes. Things don't seem to go nearly as smoothly when I try to do them in my own strength. Even the simplest of tasks are more stressful. It has left me determined not to let anything interfere with my time with Him.

Countless times over the years, I listened as fellow Christians talked about the love relationship they shared with Jesus. I tried to imagine what that was like and questioned why I didn't feel the same intimacy they described. I understand, now, it's unrealistic to expect to have an intimate relationship with someone you don't really know. After all, the more time you spend with Him, the better you know Him and what He desires. Understanding this, I have to wonder why many of us who profess to be Christians deny ourselves access to this life-changing relationship.

I would love to tell you that all has been perfect in our world since I embarked on this journey, but nothing could be further from the truth. While my search for peace was successful, it wasn't void of trials. In fact, from the moment I decided to make these changes in my walk with the Lord, mine and Rob's world was turned upside down. We entered, yet again, a time of suffering. I even wondered if another thread of loss was being woven into our tapestry.

On January 27th, just shy of a month into my search for peace, our son suffered a collapsed lung and developed a mass in his neck. One lung surgery, a chest tube, and nine days later we were sent home from the hospital for him to heal. That's when we decided to have what we thought to be a swollen lymph node in his neck evaluated. Upon further testing, the doctors concluded it was actually a mass. After being diagnosed with cancer myself, hearing the word *mass* and *my son* in the same sentence brought me to my knees. But after six months of ultrasounds and several needle aspirations, we determined it was indeed a *benign mass*. Expelling a huge sigh of relief, we then learned three months later my husband's company was downsizing and his job was going to be eliminated.

Without a doubt, 2012 was a year packed full of one test after another. However, because of the time I was spending with God, I confronted each one of these trials with a new-found perspective and strength. As we gathered in the hospital waiting for Caleb to undergo lung surgery, I had peace. Not that we wouldn't encounter complications, but peace that God was in control. While we waited for the doctors to determine whether the mass in Caleb's neck was malignant or benign, I experienced peace. Not peace that it wouldn't be cancer, rather believing if it was malignant, God was more than able to heal him. When Rob lost his job and the weeks turned into months, I experienced peace. Not that we wouldn't suffer financially, but peace knowing that God uses trials to refine us.

Over the last twelve months, to an outsider looking in, there was nothing resembling anything close to peace in our family. Still, I had peace. Peace that passes all understanding. Peace that even if my prayers aren't answered the way I want, everything will be all right. Peace that whatever God allows to happen in my life is part of His plan ... His perfect plan.

> "Peace I leave with you; my peace I give to you. Not as the world gives do I give to you. Let not your hearts be troubled, neither let them be afraid."
>
> John 14:27 (NIV)

The Dillard Family 2012

EPILOGUE
Threads of Grace

Grace: unmerited favor; the love and mercy God shows us because He desires us to have it, not because of anything we do to earn it. Threads of grace were present throughout my journey, even though I failed to see them at times.

GRACE IS A FREE GIFT offered to everyone. I think Alexander Whyte describes it perfectly when he says, "Grace, then, is grace—that is to say, it is sovereign, it is free, it is sure, it is unconditional, and it is everlasting."

God offers each of us this wonderful gift first through salvation in His son, Jesus Christ. While some of us will choose to accept this gift, others will not. It is not a one-time event in our life; rather, it grows as we mature in our relationship with the Lord.

God's abounding grace is never-ending and flows freely to all who accept it. Grace teaches us how to live. It gives us the ability to survive hardships we never imagined possible. It not only allows us to walk through the valleys of life, but enables us to rest while in the valley. It forgives. It heals the brokenhearted. Mends damaged relationships. Grace transforms lives. It offers hope to the hopeless and redeems the lost. It paid the price for your eternal life. It knows no limits and has no boundaries. It is a priceless gift. Grace.

I wish I could tell you I understood the magnitude of this amazing gift better after working on this book, but I can't. I am not sure my finite mind is able to grasp the depth and greatness of this wonderful thing called grace. However, after hours of reflection, I am able to see all the many places and times God wove this thread into my tapestry.

As I started to write, I could clearly see all the moments along my journey where I stood in need of grace, whether it was when I first came to know Christ as my Savior, or the times when I realized my relationship with Him lacked.

God's forgiving grace was present when I made choices that compromised my beliefs. When I struggled to forgive myself, He forgave me, ultimately teaching me how to forgive myself.

And when the threads of loss and grief ran so deeply throughout my life, regrettably, I saw my choice not to accept God's grace. Through all those years of disappointment and waiting, when nothing seemed to be going according to my plan, oh, how I needed His grace. And so He sent it. Many times it was the very thread holding everything in place, when my own strength was insufficient.

I saw my need for grace countless times as I sought forgiveness for my transgressions. And, just as I needed grace throughout the years, He also presented me opportunities to extend it. At times I followed His prompting, but sadly there were instances I missed the mark. During those moments, I am especially thankful His grace has no measure.

God's unmerited grace and favor was poured on Rob and me as we walked through my battle with cancer. It was a beautiful illustration of His grace continuously raining down, protecting me as well as the life of my unborn baby. He even supplied me with enough grace to accept losing my hair.

His grace abounded as He restored my health and physical body. Knowing I would soon need a spiritual restoration, He poured out more grace.

And, indeed, I felt His grace covering us as I realized we loosened our grip and began to stumble. Gently and lovingly, He nudged us back into His arms. Because of His unfailing grace, I now swap days once filled with chaos and stress for ones He brings perfect order to.

He has given me the grace to look at the trials and disappointments of this life from a different perspective. Looking for the silver lining in each hardship, I now know that in order to experience a miracle I must first walk through the fire.

But more importantly than all of this, I recognize that He transformed my life and forgave me, through His gift of redeeming grace. He restored what I broke and made it brand new in spite of my past mistakes. And He wants to do the same for you.

As if all that wasn't enough, He even supplied the grace

for me to write this book. You see, in the beginning, I merely thought I was writing an autobiography. A story about a life that has endured its fair share of trials and hardships; one that has not always taken the best route and as a result, ended up with less than God's best for me. A life that wants desperately to please God, but often fails miserably for reasons I can't explain. One that has been blessed far beyond what I deserved. A life completely unworthy of this wonderful gift called grace. And while all these things are still true, I now see it is so much more.

In retrospect, I realize this is really a story about Him. I was just blessed to be along for the ride.

> "Grace and peace be yours in abundance through the knowledge of God and Jesus our Lord."
>
> 2 Peter 1:2 (NIV)

About the Author

MELODY DILLARD IS A WIFE, mother, and interior designer. She is also a breast cancer survivor, and her story is a remarkable testimony of God's grace and faithfulness. She and her husband, Rob, have been married for more than 23 years and have two children, Caleb and Avery. Their family's 68-acre horse farm in Chesterfield, Virginia is her own little slice of heaven. She is active at The Heights Baptist Church where she helps facilitate a weekly Bible study for teenage girls.

Order this book at www.livingbyhisdesign.com or
www.facebook.com/#!/MelodyDillardASurvivorsJourney

CPSIA information can be obtained at www.ICGtesting.com
Printed in the USA
BVOW03s0202240713

326545BV00002B/5/P